MW01708782

Care
Art and Design

SEVENTH EDITION

LINDA BALL AND
NOEL CHAPMAN

KOGAN PAGE
CAREERS
SERIES

Important Notice

Please note that changes to course application procedures were being announced as this book went to press, with the merger of the Art and Design Admissions Registry (ADAR) and the Universities and Colleges Admissions Service (UCAS). The UCAS *Handbook* should be consulted regarding applications for degree courses due to start in 1997.

Acknowledgements

The authors would like to thank the past and present art and design students, the staff of art and design departments, the careers advisers in higher education, and the qualified artists and designers for their help in compiling this book.

First published in 1981
Seventh edition 1996

Apart from any fair dealing for the purposes of research or private study, or criticism or review, as permitted under the Copyright, Design and Patents Act, 1988, this publication may only be reproduced, stored or transmitted, in any form or by any means, with the prior permission in writing of the publishers, or in the case of reprographic reproduction in accordance with the terms of licences issued by the Copyright Licensing Agency. Enquiries concerning reproduction outside those terms should be sent to the publishers at the undermentioned address:

Kogan Page Limited
120 Pentonville Road
London N1 9JN

© Kogan Page Limited 1981, 1983, 1985, 1987, 1989, 1992, 1996

British Library Cataloguing in Publication Data

A CIP record for this book is available from the British Library.

ISBN: 0-7494-1762-5

Typeset by BookEns Ltd, Royston, Herts.
Printed and bound in Great Britain by Clays Ltd, St Ives plc.

Contents

Introduction **7**

Part 1

1. **Deciding on Art and Design** **11**
   Where Do Your Interests Lie? 11; Is Training Really Necessary? 11; What Kind of Course Would Suit You? 12; Will You Have to Decide on Your Specialism Right Away? 12; How Motivated Are You? 13; Who Can You Talk to about Art and Design? 15

2. **Which Subject?** **16**
   1. Creative and Performing Arts 17; 2. Fashion and Textile Design 18; 3. Fine Art 19; 4. Graphic Design and Illustration 21; 5. History of Art and Design 22; 6 Three-Dimensional Design (including interior design and theatre design) 23; 7. Other Subjects Related to Art and Design 26

3. **Which Qualification?** **27**
   Foundation Courses 28; Vocational Courses 29; What Qualifications Do Vocational Courses Lead To? 30; Professional Qualifications 32; Degree Courses 32; Postgraduate and Advanced Study 33

4. **Applying for Courses** **34**
   How and When to Apply for Courses 34; Postgraduate Study 36; Interviews 37; Grants 38; Loans 39; Mature Students 39

5. **Career Areas** **40**
General Career Prospects 40; What Are the Prospects? 41; Postgraduate Study 41; What Skills Do Artists/Designers Need to Survive After College? 42; Creative and Performing Arts 42; Fashion and Textile Design 43; Fine Art 49; Graphic Design 50; Illustration 56; History of Art 61; Three-Dimensional Design (including industrial design, product design, interior design, theatre design) 62

6. **The Practising Artist, Craftsperson and Freelance Designer** **68**
Ways of Getting Established 68; Where Will You Work? 70; Legal and Financial Problems 71; What Outlets are There for Your Work? 71; Making a Living? 73

7. **Other Careers Involving Art and Design** **75**
Arts Administration 75; Art Therapy 79; Community Arts 81; Conservation and Restoration 84; Designers in Television and Film 88; Museums and Art Galleries 89; Teaching 92

Part 2

8. **Full-Time Courses in Art and Design** **101**
BTEC and SCOTVEC 102; National Council for Vocational Qualifications 105; City & Guilds 105; Other Awards 106; RSA Examinations Board 106; Examinations Conducted by the Regional Examining Bodies 106; First Degrees in Art and Design 107; University First Degrees 108; Higher Degrees Awarded by Universities 116; Diplomas Awarded by Universities 118; Certificates awarded by Universities 120

9. **Addresses** **121**
General 121; Professional Organisations, Private Colleges and Other Useful Addresses 122; Clearing Houses for Courses 125

10. **Further Reading** **126**
Course Directories 126; Grants 126; Further Reading 127; Journals and Periodicals 128

Introduction

This book explores career opportunities in art and design and routes through art and design education in our colleges and universities.

Through art and design we can experience the opportunity to combine personal and creative development. The role of the artist and designer is constantly changing and evolving as new applications of design are discovered and the boundaries of art are rolled further forward. Despite enormous changes, mainly due to funding and economics, in the way that courses are structured and operated, art and design education in this country still offers a unique form of personal exploration, training and development, which is unlike any other programme of academic study. The range of subjects is already wide, and increasing continually. The applications are apparently limitless – from painting or conceptual art to product design, from stained glass or sculpture to computer animation.

Over recent years the importance has been recognised of having not only purely creative people but also people with other skills and abilities – people who can lead, organise, co-ordinate, direct and manage others.

Modern electronic media systems challenge the technical and creative abilities of the designer and we have in recent years seen the introduction of film, video, computer-aided design, desktop publishing and other computer applications in our courses. Art and design education responds to the needs of industry, by tradition, providing a vocational form of training to equip young designers and artists at the start of their careers.

The creative process by which artists and designers work and the skills and attributes they develop on their courses aim to prepare them for the demands of an ever-changing world. They learn to develop critical awareness, to be self-motivated, independent, flexible, open to all possibilities, and their personal development is integral to the design process or in the artefacts they produce. Whatever fields of work they enter, whether in art, design, craft or in something totally unrelated, they are equipped to make a valuable contribution to the world in which we live and work.

Even for those sure of the direction they wish their career to take, the route to achievement is not always clear. Where to start? How long does training last? What qualifications must I have? These are just some of the questions that pose themselves, and which this book aims to answer.

Part 1

Chapter 1

Deciding on Art and Design

Where Do Your Interests Lie?

You may already have very definite ideas about what you want to do: for example a sculpture course, possibly at degree level if you have the GCSEs and A levels required; or graphic design but you need to know more about the courses available. Many people begin with a general interest in art and design, with experience of only one or two areas, and would like the opportunity to try other areas of art and design before deciding which specialisation to follow.

Is Training Really Necessary?

Entering art and design inevitably means spending between two and five years or more in further and higher education. Few people manage to succeed as practising artists or designers without having been through an art or design education, and natural talent is not the only consideration; art and design education in this country has developed over the years to provide the creative, theoretical, technical and personal elements that combine to equip its graduates with the basic skills and attitudes they need to begin their careers.

Often, it is not until near completion of their courses that many people actually become aware of exactly where their true interests and abilities lie: when the full range of career opportunities opens up to them and what they require becomes apparent. The competitive world in which we work makes the possession of recognised qualifications increasingly important in all fields. When dealing in the currency of individualism and innovation, recognised qualifications provide prospective employers with a standard by which to gauge the level of your talents and abilities.

What Kind of Course Would Suit You?

You can find out more about subject choices in Chapter 2, and courses at all levels are fully described in Chapter 3. In choosing a course, consider whether you wish to follow:

An academic course, such as the history of art and design or media studies, in which you may explore the academic study of the history and appreciation of art and design subjects, without necessarily being involved in the practice.

A course which combines the practice with the study of art and design, as do many of the degree courses in art colleges, colleges of higher education, and some universities; and higher diploma courses in art and design. The academic content of art and design courses is usually the study of the theory, history and appreciation of art and design, and related subjects.

A course where there is little or no academic content and a high proportion of practical work. Many vocational art and design courses do not specifically include academic study. The academic content of the history of art and design and complementary studies will vary from course to course, and you should read the prospectus and entry requirements carefully for each course before applying. However little academic study there is, you will find *all* courses include technical and theoretical studies to support the practical work.

A combined course, either combining subjects within art and design, such as a multi-disciplinary degree course which may offer three-dimensional studies with graphics, textiles and supporting studies; or combining art and design with other subjects, such as design with business studies; fine art with Italian.

A specialist course. There are some courses which concentrate on the practice and study of specialised aspects of art and design in depth. These courses exist at vocational, degree and advanced level, eg in film, TV, photography; stained glass design; product design; or musical instrument technology, for example.

Will You Have to Decide on Your Specialism Right Away?

If you decide to go directly into further or higher education you will obviously need to make choices about your specialism. For most people this is far too early to make such a major decision: they are neither informed enough of the options nor sufficiently aware of personal capabilities and long-term interests.

Despite the recent increases in direct-entry applications (often driven by students wishing to reduce the financial costs of their education by decreasing its time span), students are generally encouraged to do a Foundation course or a one-year General Art and Design BTEC course. Since the introduction of GNVQs, these are now designed to carry on directly from GCSE-level studies. Foundation courses are either of one or two years' duration and run by most local art and design colleges. Students are not normally eligible for a grant, but fees are usually paid.

BTEC National Diploma courses in General Art and Design are full-year courses; grants and awards may be discretionary. Run similarly are BTEC First Diploma courses, which are designed for those without formal entry qualifications to other higher level courses. These courses offer the opportunity to test out areas you have not yet explored, as well as areas that are familiar to you. However, beware! Even on a year's course, time is short; and if you are preparing for entry to degree or vocational courses in the following year, you will need to decide your chief area of study at the end of the first term, at Christmas, or early in the spring term, so that there is time to prepare relevant work for your portfolio to take along to interviews. If you still don't wish to specialise after the Foundation course there are many general art and design courses and multi-disciplinary degrees where you can pursue more than one interest.

How Motivated Are You?

Following on with a subject that you are good at? 'Art is my best subject at school, so it seems a natural move to go on to art college.' Even if it is your best subject you may not measure up to the standards expected at art college. Enjoying art at school is one thing, but are you sufficiently devoted to follow art and design or an aspect of it for up to three or four years in higher education? Are you prepared to take on the academic and theoretical work involved? Why not seek your art teacher's opinion about your abilities? After all, he or she had an art education too and should be able to give you some honest feedback about your talents and potential and some guidance as to the most suitable course. Also, it is often possible to arrange an advisory interview at your local art college when you can have a chat with a tutor and show some of your work. In any case, visit your local art college on Open Days and during the summer degree and diploma shows, when you will get a chance to talk to students and see a wide range of art and design on display.

As a 'soft' option? 'An art and design degree will be less demanding than other academic degree courses, and I find art a lot easier.' Many people are under the mistaken impression that art is an easy option, a means of escaping from academic work. This is one popular myth that needs to be challenged! In any case it is rather a negative reason for choosing the subject, and your lack of positive interest would certainly be revealed at an interview. Whatever course you choose to follow, the demands made on you are considerable, creatively, technically and intellectually, and particularly so on the degree courses. There are few courses where you will be solely concerned with practical work, and all have structures and timetables, some more rigorous than others. Many require a high degree of self-motivation on the part of the student who has to generate, organise and plan his/her own work – and creative inspiration rarely comes to order! The freedoms are a challenge in themselves.

Technical and theoretical studies are vital to support a student's practical work. Assessments are regular, as they are for any kind of course, and many include exams and essays as well as discussions, assessments and critiques of your work with tutors and examiners. The expected intellectual and academic requirements are reflected in minimum entry qualifications which are similar to other subjects in higher education, many requiring GCSEs and A levels or equivalents in academic subjects. Entry requirements for courses are explained in Chapter 3.

As a way of training for a specific occupation? Some people choose art and design because they have specific career intentions: to become an illustrator, an interior designer, practising artist – and they see the course as a natural step on the route to achieving their goal. For some occupations it is essential to complete a course before gaining entry to a job. (See Chapter 5.)

For job security? 'I chose my art and design course because at least there's a job at the end of it.' When choosing a course, remember there is no *guarantee* of a job at the end of it, whatever you study. The job market is always unpredictable, and your qualifications are not the only factors to be evaluated by employers when entering the job market. Your skills and talents, general suitability for the job, your personality, appearance, your ability to fit in, the geographical areas in which you are looking, and the general competitiveness of the job market are all going to feature in your search for a job.

For personal satisfaction? Not all students are concerned about their employment prospects, seeing an art and design course as a way of exploring an area in depth and for their own personal development. Many tutors and students will say this is the best reason for wanting to do a course because you value the opportunity to spend time exploring new freedoms, extending your creative and intellectual skills, acquiring knowledge of techniques, new skills, styles and approaches to your work, and finding your own direction through your artwork.

Who Can You Talk to about Art and Design?

Talking to other people about your career plans is a good way of testing your motivations. Parents, teachers, friends and careers officers may encourage or dissuade you from choosing art and design. If you can resist these pressures successfully you will prove to yourself and to others that you are sufficiently motivated.

Chapter 2
Which Subject?

There were, on the last count, possibly 100 different subject titles in art and design, from wildlife illustration to weaving, and from knitwear design to fine art. Some courses are geared to the needs of specific industries, some may be very technical; others place a greater emphasis on artistic expression and creativity, and some may have a high academic content. Lists of courses may be found in Part 2.

In order to examine each area in more detail, art and design is divided under the headings listed below:

1. Creative and Performing Arts – combined courses with theatre, music, dance, the visual arts.
2. Fashion and Textiles – including embroidery, footwear, knitting, woven and printing textiles.
3. Fine Art – painting, sculpture, printmaking.
4. Graphic Design and Illustration.
5. History of Art and Design; Film and Media Studies.
6. Three-Dimensional Design – interior design, industrial and product design, wood, ceramics, furniture, silversmithing, jewellery, metal, plastics, glass.
7. Other subjects related to art and design – education degrees (BEd); combined courses; film, photography, television.

Boundaries between areas can be vague or even overlap. For example, graphics students may work in three dimensions, three-dimensional design students may do painting – so don't expect to find courses are narrow. In addition, there are some multi-disciplinary and combined courses where more than one subject area may be studied: for example, a degree in three-dimensional design with graphics and textiles.

An increasingly wide range of options is offered within courses as the influences and applications of art and design grow. For example, at most colleges graphic design now includes computer graphics as applied to design for television and film as well as typography and image manipulation. You may find computers feature in fine arts courses.

As complementary studies, many art and design students do drama, dance and movement, read psychology, economics, social studies, business studies, literature – and an unlimited range of other options, depending on the course.

The study of the history of art and design, more usually called 'complementary studies' or 'design theories', forms an integral part of all art and design degree courses, Foundation courses and most vocational courses. Art and design is not, therefore, purely practical, creative and technical. A great deal of importance is placed on the practice of art and design in the light of historical and critical studies from early movements and periods in art and architecture to the study of contemporary artists and designers.

1. Creative and Performing Arts

Creative and performing arts courses are mostly offered at degree level. In the past, the study of music, drama and theatre arts, dance and the visual arts in higher education was taught as individual courses, often in specialised institutions such as colleges of dance or music, or on teacher-training courses. The boundaries between different forms of artistic expression in the performance and visual arts have become less well defined over the years; dance and drama are closely related, as are music and movement, the visual arts and music – and so on. Creative and performing arts courses have emerged as an exciting way of exploring, at an academic and practical level, one or more of the disciplines and relationships between the different forms of expression.

The combinations of subjects offered vary, as can be seen from the list of courses in Part 2. For example, at one college, theatre studies and music only are offered, while at another you can choose options from English with creative writing, theatre studies, music, dance and the visual arts.

The Main Constituent Areas

Visual arts – not just drawing and painting, but could also include sculpture, three-dimensional design or crafts, such as wood or ceramics, printmaking, photography and film, graphics, textiles, and supporting theoretical and historical studies.

Theatre/drama – can include not only practical work through performance and workshop sessions, but historical studies; technical back-up; stage management; lighting and effects; costume; creative writing.

Music – most students are musically qualified in one or more orchestral or solo instruments, such as the violin, oboe or piano. Some courses offer greater flexibility and students may be using modern instruments such as electric guitars and keyboard instruments, and electronic music. Music will normally be supported by theoretical and historical studies.

Dance – practical and technical aspects– choreography, dance composition, improvisation, movement studies, historical studies in dance; the use of music, costume, theatrical effects; exploration and study of styles from classical ballet to modern dance; uses of production workshops prevalent throughout; interrelation with drama, music etc.

Other options – one course offers arts administration; another, English with creative writing. Some courses place an emphasis on community involvement and students may become involved with local community arts activities during their courses.

At interview, students are expected to give evidence of their creative abilities and present a folio of recent work, if applying for visual arts.

Students opting for drama, music or dance will almost certainly be expected to prepare a piece for audition. The academic content of the courses is fairly high, and the intellectual development of the students is as important as it would be for any other academic degree course. Outside their course studies, students are expected regularly to attend concerts, theatrical productions, dance or ballet and visit art galleries, to complement their studies.

2. Fashion and Textile Design

Fashion and textile design courses exist at all levels of qualification – Foundation, vocational, degree and postgraduate. There are normally chief studies in two main areas: *fashion design* – garment and accessory design; and *textile design, printed, knitted or woven* – for fashion or furnishing and decorative use, ie furnishing fabrics, wall hangings, curtain fabrics, etc. The fashion designer requires an understanding of textiles and their uses. The textile designer must be aware of the applications of fabrics in clothing and decorative areas. Some courses combine fashion and textile design as a chief study.

The courses involve creative, academic and technical aspects: for example, general design studies, professional design practice, techniques such as weaving, printing and dyeing, pattern design and cutting, sewing skills, machine and hand-knitted fabrics and clothing.

There are some courses in the fashion and textile area which are devoted solely to one subject for specialised study: eg, embroidery; design of carpets and related textiles; and knitwear design. Some courses are completely broad based and simply entitled 'Surface pattern' or such. Some courses also offer business or management studies, including marketing, accounts, commerce, and economics. Fashion promotion, retailing and journalism are recent additions to the range of courses available. Some courses are four years long with industrial placements in relevant companies in the UK and abroad!

These courses prepare students for many different careers in the fashion and textiles and related industries in design, production, promotion, management or publishing. Many work freelance or in small textile design studios and consultancies.

3. Fine Art

Fine art courses are most commonly offered at degree level, so the description below relates chiefly to the content of BA degrees at art colleges and some universities.

What is fine art? Various course brochures describe their courses in the following ways: 'chief studies in painting, fine printmaking, or sculpture. Encourages the discovery of the nature of the student's talent by imaginative use of a wide variety of available facilities based on a personal work programme.' 'An open situation wherein any form of enquiry into perceptual expression is allowable and where students may evolve and design their own terms of their visual language.' 'An enquiry into relationships between elements, objects space ...' One students view: 'I followed a fine art degree, and although I shall probably end up doing some totally unrelated job, I feel the luxury of being able to spend three years exploring myself and my ideas through my artwork has been an exciting and fulfilling experience and is something I shall always value.'

What Can You Do within Fine Art?

Most fine art departments offer: painting; sculpture – in a whole range of materials; printmaking – silkscreen, lithography, etching, film, video, photography and other materials/media. Some departments may expect you to choose one area to specialise in, while others will give you the opportunity to work in all three. Whichever area you choose, there will be a considerable amount of drawing and supporting studies to complement your main subject. You might want to work in ceramics, wood, cement, stone or fibreglass, but it is important to stress that you will not be receiving training as a craftsperson. Instruction in basic techniques and use of tools and equipment may be taught but creativity and freedom of expression with the materials is the chief aim. Film, video or photography facilities are available to most art and design students, and in some departments it is possible to choose one of these as a major area of creative study.

History and theory of art is an extremely important aspect of most fine art courses, which believe that it is essential for you to study the major art movements, including contemporary art, in order to gain an understanding of the development of art and how this may relate to your own creativity. All fine art courses will have a structure, but within that there may be tremendous freedom to explore things in depth and organise your own work programme: a high degree of self-motivation is required. Some courses offer a fairly general first year, allowing students to experiment in all the main areas, and within these to explore different methods and styles of approach to their work. In their final two or three years students may then choose a chief area of study in which to specialise.

What of the career prospects? Most students are aware that there are no recognised vocational ends and see the course as an intellectual and creative exercise in its own right, possibly in the same way as would a student of philosophy or other non-vocational academic degree subject. Many potential fine art students are discouraged by parents, friends, teachers and others who see no obvious vocation except that of a struggling, practising artist. For this reason students are often directed (or direct themselves) towards graphics, illustration or other design courses, in the belief that these will offer a 'better' guarantee of employment. But far from emerging from college as unemployable misfits, information collected by art colleges and other surveys has shown that fine art leavers enter a wide range of jobs and occupations both related and unrelated to art and design (see Chapter 5).

4. Graphic Design and Illustration

Graphic design is to do with visual communication. A number of different disciplines can fall under the broad heading of graphic design: design studies, film and animation work, typography and lettering, illustration, printing processes and printmaking, display and exhibition work, technical graphics for engineering, calligraphy, model-making, packaging, design for advertising and so on.

Design itself is normally the chief area of study, where the student, through theory and practice, learns the basic principles of design, explores the elements of visual communication and spends a substantial amount of time on drawing. On some courses it is possible to pursue a specialist subject throughout, such as illustration or typography, or to specialise during the second and third years, for example choosing options in advertising design, photography and film, typography, packaging, illustration (even medical and scientific), and exhibition design. The uses and application of modern technology including computers are increasingly a feature of courses. Film, TV and video are increasingly offered in graphic design courses.

Graphic design work is not necessarily always in two dimensions. Many students do three-dimensional studies, particularly where this is applied to model-making, packaging, exhibition design, or display. Technical and professional skills are taught as an integral part of the course. Problem-solving – the visualising of ideas and solutions to design problems – is a continuing process throughout the course. A high level of creative and technical excellence is achieved, as can be seen by the work displayed at finals college shows.

The study of the history of art and supporting or complementary studies comprises at least 15–20 per cent of degree courses and will feature on most other kinds of course in graphic design. Within this, graphics students may be able to study the history of design and illustration, for example. Their studies in relation to visual communications also might include psychology, and social and economic issues.

Students are encouraged to have a professional approach to their work, as would be expected of a qualified designer working in commerce, industry and other areas. The structure of courses at degree, vocational and Foundation level will be geared to project-based work, working to a set 'brief', and meeting deadlines. For example, a theme for a design project may be a 'health education' campaign – and within that, students may be asked to produce a series of designs for posters, handbills and magazines advertising. Within the brief, there may be restrictions with regard to the budget available, printing facilities, range of colours used, deadline to be met, and so on. On degree courses particularly, tutors may encourage students to design their own work programmes, set their own projects, topics and deadlines, the emphasis being on self-directed study. Professional studies will be fundamental to all courses and will cover aspects such as how to approach and deal with clients, how to respond to a brief, how to present work to clients, printing requirements and limitations, and gaining familiarity with the jargon used.

In recent years there has been a growth in courses or course components offering electronic media, film, video and computer applications to graphic art and design. However, most employers of designers will tell you that the basic skills of drawing, typography and layout continue to be essential to a designer's training.

5. History of Art and Design

Your interest may be in appreciation, criticism and history rather than participating in creative artistic activity yourself. The history of art and design can be studied as an academic degree, and also features as an integral part of degree, Foundation and many vocational courses in art and design.

Let us take, first, the history of art and design as an academic course in its own right. (Some courses are purely the study of the history of art; others encompass history of design too. There are also one or two fairly new courses which are solely concerned with the history of design.) Universities and colleges offer BA degrees in this range of subjects. In the universities particularly, the history of art and design may be offered with other subsidiary or joint academic subjects, such as languages, history, literature, and so on. Most courses concentrate on the study of Western European art, its painting, sculpture and architecture, but some offer studies in Latin American art, Ancient Greek and Roman art, or the history of film and cinema. Others may devote considerable time to the study of the history of design in the 19th and 20th centuries.

Second, let us look at the history of art and design as part of an art and design degree, Foundation and vocational courses. One of the myths attached to art and design courses is that they are practical and therefore an easier option to pursue than academic courses. Most tutors and art students will tell you that the demands, both creative and academic, are considerable, and that it is by no means a soft option! In universities and art colleges, the academic study of the history of art and complementary studies must amount to at least 15 per cent of the course content, while in university art and design degrees, it may be more. Most vocational and Foundation courses in art and design include the study of the history of art and design as an important part of the course. Whether you choose fine art, graphics, ceramics, fashion, or any of the other art and design subjects, you will find that history of art and design studies will support and complement your creative work. For example, graphics students will most probably study the history of design, and fashion students may examine popular culture.

6. Three-Dimensional Design

(including interior design and theatre design)

Courses in three-dimensional studies are offered at all levels, from Foundation to postgraduate, at a wide range of colleges and institutions all over the country. Overall, this area of art and design is concerned with the creation of designs in three dimensions. These can be functional objects, such as furniture, product designs and jewellery, and also sculptural and non-functional forms in wood, ceramics, glass, etc.

The disciplines include: chief studies in furniture design, wood, glass, metal, ceramics, plastics, jewellery, silversmithing, industrial design – with an engineering bias – and product design – often working in one or more of the above materials. Interior design and theatre design are also offered and are dealt with separately below.

The approaches to working in three dimensions vary: one course may offer chief studies in industrial design, which is closely allied to engineering, and includes technological studies and may have a maths GCSE or equivalent entry requirement. Another course may offer studies in ceramics where students are concentrating on free artistic expression, and experiment through working with their materials, producing functional or decorative forms. Some colleges may offer single degree or vocational course subjects such as furniture or interior design. Others may offer the study of more than one area and combine, say, wood, metal, ceramics, plastics and glass. Another alternative is a course which is general in the first year and then gives students the opportunity to specialise in the second and third years. Some courses are specifically geared towards design for commercial production; others may attract students who wish to pursue work as individual artist-craftspeople, designing and making objects in their own studios.

Interior Design

Interior design is concerned with the design of living, working and leisure space inside buildings. This can include colour schemes, the selection of materials for walls, floors, ceilings, the selection of furniture and fabrics and the design of fixtures and fittings themselves.

Interior design courses sometimes have common course components with architecture courses, while others could be linked with retail display and exhibition design. Courses will include creative, technical and professional design elements. One student says: 'Our course is geared to professional practice, and includes the study of architectural principles too. We also study psychology and the history of art and design. Drawing ability is really important. If you can't draw designs and present them beautifully, you are in for a hard time. We work to briefs as would any designer in professional practice.'

Theatre Design

This is offered at a limited number of institutions as a chief study at degree and vocational level. This is one student's experience: 'We do design projects, ie reading a play and designing a set with drawings and a 3D model. Fine art studies, drawing, painting, and so on, are done as supporting studies. The first year includes a lot of groundwork: blocks of time spent on costume-making, set and properties construction, woodwork, scene painting, and lighting. The rest of the course is spent doing design projects with some fieldwork with outside theatres. We also study history of art and history of theatre and costumes, and of course playwrights. We finish with one major design for a public performance.'

Costume for Stage, Screen, Film and Television

Courses are designed specifically for students willing to pursue careers as costume designers, interpreters or supervisors of costume within the film, theatre and television industries. Many costume designers and wardrobe designers now working in those industries came from fashion backgrounds, particularly those specialising in contemporary (ie non-period) work. You may find it helpful to consult *Careers in Fashion* (Kogan Page).

Media, Film, Photography and Television

These subjects may feature on many art and design courses as supporting studies, and at some colleges can also be chosen as a main option in, for example, a graphic design degree course. Media studies, film, photography, television, video and specialised courses such as documentary film-making and film animation, and TV graphics also exist as degree and vocational courses in their own right.

A number of courses exist for those interested in the broader aspects of television, video and theatre design, where management and production are also studied. Some courses mix film history and cultural studies, under such fashionable titles as media studies, lens-based media, or such. Carefully cross-reference the ADAR (Art and Design Admissions Registry) Handbook *On Course* to find a course that offers the areas of study closest to your particular interest.

Foundation courses will usually include short courses in the use of camera and photographic techniques and may offer film, TV and photography as study areas. These areas are beyond the scope of this book and further details are given in *Careers in*

Television and Radio, published by Kogan Page. Lists of courses at all levels are produced by the British Institute of Professional Photography and the British Film Institute. See also *Education and Training for Film and Television,* published by the British Kinematograph, Sound and Television Society.

7. Other Subjects Related to Art and Design

Education Degrees with Art and Design as a Main Subject (BEd)

Training for teaching after completion of an art and design degree is discussed in Chapter 7. However, there are other routes to becoming qualified as a teacher. One way is to follow a BEd (Bachelor of Education) degree course which is a three- or four-year training in education theory and practice for entry into the teaching profession. Art and design is offered as a main or subsidiary subject in many colleges running such courses. However, a BA in Art and Design concentrates more time on the pursuit of art and design for its own sake. Then, should you decide to enter teaching, the BA may be followed by a one-year postgraduate course which qualifies you to teach in schools and further education (see pp 92–7). The BEd route may be shorter if you intend to teach, though you are likely to achieve a more intensive art training following a BA in Art and Design, followed by the one-year postgraduate teacher training course ATC or PGCE (see pp 93–4).

Those completing a course of teacher training are expected to have GCSE level passes at grade C or above in English language and maths.

Combined Courses

Some courses exist where you can study more than one art and design subject. These may be called combined or multi-disciplinary courses, eg three-dimensional design and graphics, or general courses including all or many art and design subjects. Art and design subjects may also be combined with other academic subjects, such as fine art and languages, business studies and design (see Part 2).

Chapter 3

Which Qualification?

This chapter looks at the qualifications offered in art and design subjects and tells you about the entry requirements. The details of how and when to apply for courses are explained in Chapter 4.

Most of the qualifications listed below require full-time study. Yet, BTEC National Certificates and Higher National Certificates offer the opportunity to study on a part-time basis usually while in a relevant occupation. A few universities and art institutions are now offering degree level courses in art and design on a part-time basis, and these may be of interest to those with home/family commitments, or those looking for an alternative to full-time study.

The qualifications are:

- □ Foundation courses
- □ BTEC Ordinary Diplomas and Certificates, Higher National Diplomas and Certificates
- □ Professional qualifications
- □ Diploma in Higher Education
- □ Degrees
- □ Postgraduate and advanced study.

General National Vocational Qualifications – GNVQs – are new alternatives to GCE A Level study or more GCSEs.

- □ Advanced GNVQs – the new 'vocational A levels' – are equivalent to two GCE A Levels, and normally take two years' full-time study.
- □ Intermediate GNVQs are equivalent to four or five GCSEs at grades A–C, and normally take one year full-time.
- □ Foundation GNVQs are equivalent to four GCSEs at grades D–G, and normally take one year of full-time study.

You can take a full GNVQ along with other qualifications – such as a GCE A Level, AS courses, a couple of GCSEs or additional GNVQ units.

- □ They are awarded by the Business and Technology Education Council (BTEC), City and Guilds (C&G) and the RSA Examinations Board (RSA). They build on the best of their existing courses, which they will soon replace.

Foundation Courses

Most degree and some vocational courses require students to have completed a Foundation course, though those with at least two A levels or GNVQ equivalents (and an impressive portfolio) may be exempted by the college (except in Scotland, where Foundation studies are included in full-time vocational and degree courses). Foundation courses give a broad education in the basic elements as preparation for entry to further training on degree and vocational courses. They also enable students to test out their commitment to the subject before embarking on a full-time course for a further three or four years.

Many applicants have limited experience of the wide range of subjects available. For example, they may have had little or no experience of working in sculpture, printmaking, textiles or three-dimensional subjects in their art training so far. Therefore a Foundation course provides the opportunity for students to be introduced to working in a wide range of materials, often for the first time, and helps them to diagnose their main specialist area.

For those who leave school at 16, the two-year Foundation course is probably more suitable and may also include study for further GCSE or GNVQ subjects – which the applicant may need in order to have the basic entry qualifications for a further course. Many applicants to one-year Foundation courses have had a sixth-form education, including A levels.

Entry Requirements

2-year Foundation course	Minimum age 16; general education; some specify GCSE Grade 3 passes or equivalent.
1-year Foundation course	Minimum age 17; general education; five GCSE Grade 3 passes or equivalent; some also prefer at least one A level subject; or GNVQ equivalent.

Each applicant will normally be called for interview, with their portfolio which gives evidence of artistic/design ability.

Although Foundation studies generally provide an excellent grounding for entry to further courses, there are some points worth noting. On one-year courses particularly, you will find that the time you have for testing out your abilities, developing new skills, and working in new areas is in fact quite short. If you decide to apply for university degree courses in art and design for the following year, you will have to reach your decision about your main subject choice half-way through your first term – as applications have to be completed by mid-December (the *UCAS Handbook* has details of late applications) and your portfolio may be sent off for inspection by the middle of January. In any case, many one-year Foundation courses like you to state a preference for a subject area before you begin – although you may be able to change your mind later – but you will have the opportunity to work in other areas during the year. You will probably be required to decide on your specialist subject by the beginning of your second term at the latest, in order to prepare a portfolio in good time for interviews in spring for UCAS degrees and vocational courses. This can be frustrating for students who, ideally, would have liked more time to spend looking at different areas of art and design.

One solution is to apply for a general or combined course after Foundation. Another is to take a year off between your Foundation course and degree/vocational course to give you more time to decide, but this could just be putting off your decision.

Finally, completion of a Foundation course *does not guarantee* you a place on a degree or vocational course, either at the same college or at colleges in other parts of the country. Competition for places on courses is often very fierce. Some of the more popular courses and colleges may receive up to four or more applications for each place.

As an alternative to Foundation studies at 16+, applicants without the minimum entry requirements may apply for BTEC National Diplomas.

Vocational Courses

Vocational courses in art and design provide chiefly professional and practical training in art and design subjects, as opposed to the more academic approach of degrees in art and design. Most vocational students attend courses in their own locality, since few local authorities will make awards for such courses outside their area, whereas degree students are eligible for a mandatory grant wherever they choose to study. The *Grants* Section in Chapter 4 explains the situation more fully. However, if you wish to do a specialised vocational course which is *not* offered at colleges in your area, your local education authority may consider supporting you to go elsewhere.

Vocational courses cover a wide range of subjects, and at present lead to a variety of qualifications including those offered by professional organisations (see p 32). Some are designed to develop skills which will give entry to many fields of employment and are often, therefore, geared to the needs of industry. Finally, there are some specialist subjects which are offered only on vocational courses, for example, documentary photography, exhibition and museum design, and stained glass design.

What Qualifications Do Vocational Courses Lead To?

BTEC Courses

There are now over 400 art and design courses at 135 colleges all over the UK, offering nationally recognised qualifications called BTEC National Diplomas and Certificates, and BTEC Higher National Diplomas and Certificates approved by the Design Board for the Business and Technology Education Council. In addition, there are BTEC courses leading to First Diplomas (one year full-time and two years part-time) and First Certificates (one year part-time), open to applicants without the minimum entry requirement for National level courses. The aim of BTEC is to offer employment-related courses in art and design studies to complement the existing provision of degree courses. The standards are high and because employers have been involved in designing the content of the courses, there is more practical experience, more day-to-day working in firms and on practical projects. Subjects include:

Visual communication. Including graphic design, illustration, technical illustration, typography, photography, audio-visual studies, advertising design, information design.

Fashion textiles and surface patterns.
Three-dimensional design. Including industrial design, interior design, design crafts, display design, exhibition design, theatre design.

Multi-disciplinary design. Diagnostic courses in art and design, conservation and restoration craft courses.

Diplomas are more advanced than Certificates which offer part-time study for those already working in design posts. It is possible to progress from a Diploma to a Higher Diploma which offers an advanced specialist training for a further two year.

Entry Requirements

16+ yrs:	BTEC First Diploma/ Certificate:	No formal entry requirements
16+ yrs:	BTEC Ordinary National Diploma/Certificate:	4 GCSE grade C or above passes or equivalent
18+ yrs:	BTEC Higher National Diploma/Certificate:	An appropriate BTEC National Award or Foundation course *and/or* 4/5 GCSE grade C or above passes *plus* 1 A level pass or GNVQ.

Length of courses: Certificates, two years part-time; Diplomas, two years full-time, three years part-time or sandwich study.

In Scotland the Scottish Vocational Education Council (SCOTVEC) offers two-year National and Higher National Diploma courses with equivalent entry requirements to BTEC courses.

Other Vocational Courses

There are vocational courses still awaiting validation under the BTEC scheme. These may at present be qualifications awarded by the colleges themselves, such as a two-year college diploma in design. Entry requirements are broadly similar to those for BTEC courses (see above). Additionally there are qualifications awarded by City and Guilds, and many colleges award professional qualifications.

Professional Qualifications

A large proportion of art education aims to train students for employment in specific professional areas of art and design. Some courses, particularly at vocational level, were set up with the approval of industries or professions which have been consulted with regard to course content and aims. It is possible, therefore, to win two qualifications at the end of the course – an educational one and a professional one – which may be awarded after a special exam or by completing a further year at the end of the course or, in some cases, simply by completing the college course satisfactorily.

The entry requirements for these courses may be agreed jointly by the college and the professional association concerned as the minimum for entrance to a particular profession. Some of the professional qualifications associated with art and design are:

CSD	– Chartered Society of Designers
LSDC	– Licentiate of the Society of Designer Craftsmen
ABID	– Associateship of the British Institute of Interior Design
BDS	– British Display Society
ATI	– Associateship of the Textile Institute.

Degree Courses

Degrees are offered by individual universities, art colleges, colleges of higher education and certain other institutions. These are normally three-year full-time courses leading to a BA, a BA(Hons), and in one case a Bachelor of Fine Art (BFA), in art and design subjects. Some four-year MA and BA sandwich courses also exist.

Polytechnics, art colleges, some colleges of higher education and other institutions previously had their degree courses approved by the Council for National Academic Awards (CNAA), which has been disbanded, and these institutions were offered the opportunity to apply for university status and, like the 'old' or traditional universities, were given the right of self-validation. Many colleges which did not apply for university status had their courses validated by another university. Degrees in art and design are normally: minimum age 18 on 31 December of the year in which the course begins, and successful completion of a

Foundation course. Minimum academic qualifications are five GCSE Grade 3 passes; or three GCSE Grade 3 passes plus one A level pass or equivalents; or two GCSE Grade 3 and two A level passes (or Scottish equivalents). For those who have not completed a Foundation course, minimum academic requirements may be at least two A level passes, GNVQ equivalents, plus O levels. Completion of other qualifications such as BTEC Diplomas and Certificates is acceptable, but it is wise to check with individual institutions.

The academic requirements listed here are the minimum, and many applicants to degree courses now have to achieve two A levels. But unqualified mature applicants, those with unusual qualifications, and those with no recent formal qualifications who have outstanding creative ability may be accepted for degree courses in the history of art and design as a main degree subject. The minimum academic requirements are two A levels and five GCSEs, or three A levels and four GCSEs or equivalents.

Postgraduate and Advanced Study

Postgraduate and advanced courses are offered in a wide range of subjects. The entry requirements are normally completion of a first degree, though some courses will accept vocational and professional qualifications. Courses lead to certificates and diplomas, or to higher degrees such as MA, MPhil, PhD. Postgraduate study falls into two distinct areas: the first extends your art education, perhaps specialising in one particular field, eg illustration, sculpture, furniture; the second comprises courses which equip you for entry to special occupations, such as art teaching, art therapy, arts administration, normally adding a professional year to your first degree qualification.

Chapter 4

Applying for Courses

How and When to Apply for Courses

You may have to apply almost a whole academic year in advance for courses in art and design. Below is a table showing when and how you should apply. This is followed by some ideas on how to prepare for interviews, information about grants, and some notes for mature applicants thinking of entering art and design. The pros and cons of deferred entry are discussed at the end of the chapter.

Most courses begin in the autumn. Dates and times given below refer to the academic year ***preceding*** the year of entry to courses. Addresses of clearing houses, who process applications, are to be found in Chapter 9.

Foundation and Vocational Courses in Art and Design

1-year and 2-year courses

Write to your local education authority at the Education Office, asking for details of their courses, and then apply direct to the colleges in which you are interested. You will probably be called for an interview and asked to bring a portfolio of your work.

When to apply: (Normally to your local art college) autumn to spring. Some popular courses are full by January, so be sure to apply in good time. No final closing date.

Method of application: Application forms from the college(s) to which forms are returned direct.

Degree Courses and BTEC Higher National Diplomas in Art and Design

When to apply: 31 March.*

** or latest date by which applications must be received.*

Method of application: A central clearing scheme deals with applications for both types of course. If you are not at college, obtain forms from the Art and Design Admissions Registry (ADAR). Some Scottish institutions also use ADAR: Duncan of Jordanstone College of Art, Falkirk College of Technology, James Watt College and Telford College. The other Scottish institutions do not use ADAR though the ADAR handbook may list some of their courses and you will need to apply to them directly. ADAR will be merged with UCAS from 1997/98 so applications for 1997 must be made to UCAS. Check with UCAS *Handbook* for new arrangements.

Registration fee. Only *two* choices of courses and 'pool'. Forms returned to ADAR by Foundation college, or by you if you are an external candidate. First choice interviews *early April*. Second choice *mid-May* onwards.

University Degrees in Art and Design (not covered by ADAR)

When to apply:* Oxford: UCAS *15th October*, and college entrance form by *30th September* (for Ruskin School). All other universities: UCAS *15 December*; by mid-January send portfolio to London.

Method of application: Application forms from your own school or college or direct from UCAS.

Registration fee. Up to *six* choices. There is a Portfolio Inspection Scheme for most Fine Art (old university) degrees. Your portfolio is sent to a centre in London. Obtain details of Inspection Scheme from your first choice university. Interviews normally *mid-February* onwards.

Other University Degrees

ie, History of Art

When to apply:* UCAS closing date *15th December*; Oxbridge *15th October*. Interviews in spring.

Other Degrees at Colleges of Higher Education

When to apply:* Autumn onwards. No final closing date. Popular courses fill up quickly, though some may accept applications later in the year.

** or latest date by which applications must be received.*

Method of application: Application forms from the college(s) to which forms are returned direct. Interviews throughout the year.

NB: For BEd degrees and some combined courses, a central clearing scheme deals with applications. The prospectus should tell you this. Obtain forms and lists of degrees in the scheme from the Central Register and Clearing House.

Registration fee. Up to *six* choices. Interviews December onwards.

If in doubt about which scheme your degree course falls into, the course prospectus should tell you. Applicants may apply to degree courses in all schemes if they wish.

Postgraduate Study
Higher Degrees and Diplomas in Art and Design

When to apply:* Forms available beginning of January. To be returned not later than end of *January*.

Method of application: Application forms from your own college, or if you have already left, obtain direct from UCAS.

Registration fee. *Two* choices. If still at college, forms and confidential report to be sent by your college to first choice postgraduate centre. Other candidates send forms and report to UCAS. First choice interviews – *February*. Second choice – *mid-March*.

Other Higher Degrees, Diplomas, Certificates at Universities and Colleges

When to apply:* *December* onwards. Many institutions have closing dates for postgraduate applications in the spring.

Method of application: Application forms from postgraduate course to which they must be returned. Interviews normally spring and early summer.

Royal College of Art, Master of Arts/Master of Design

When to apply:* Closing dates *January* onwards, except for Painting, when students apply in *August* after they have left college for entry in one academic year's time.

* *or latest date by which applications must be received.*

Method of application: College entrance exam. Apply through your first degree college or if you have left – apply direct.

Postgraduate Art Teachers' Certificate/Diploma
1 year

When to apply: mid-October.*
Method of application: Registration fee. *Three* choices. Application forms from your own department if still at college. If not, obtain direct from: The Clearing House for Postgraduate Courses in Art Education.

Postgraduate Certificate in Education (PGCE)
When to apply:* October onwards of year prior to entry.

Method of application: Clearing scheme. Registration fee. Forms from Graduate Teacher Training Registry. Up to *six* choices.

Interviews

Your motivation, your interest in the subject and the college, your suitability for the course, your abilities and your portfolio are all taken into account. It is important to prepare for the interview by finding out as much as you can about the college, the course content, methods of tuition and assessment, facilities, options and subject choices. Open Days will give you the opportunity to talk to students and staff and look round. At some colleges, particularly at postgraduate level, you may be required to do an entrance test or exam.

The style of the interview will vary from college to college. At one you may be interviewed in a group along with other applicants, while at another you may talk individually with tutors. Whatever the policy, you will be asked to talk about your work and to show that you are fairly sure in your own mind about doing that particular course. Beforehand, you should find someone who can help you prepare for the interview, by selecting work, and discussing the questions you should ask.

* *or latest date by which applications must be received.*

Grants

The grants position for many students is at present uncertain, owing to cuts in local authority budgets. Some LEAs are restricting the number and type of awards given to students. It is essential that you find out early on about your eligibility for an award and the kind of grant you may receive. You should make a grant application to your LEA in the spring *even* if you have not yet been accepted on to a course. Many LEAs like to receive grant applications by the *end of March* for entry to courses the following year.

Here is a rough guide to the current grant position for most of the art and design courses.

Discretionary award. This means that the LEA is not obliged to give you an award and if they do, the amount may vary according to how the LEA views the course. Travel awards are also discretionary.

Mandatory awards. This means that the LEA is obliged to give you a major award for post A-level, ie further education courses, provided that you are eligible in all other respects.

Foundation Courses

Discretionary. Many LEAs will not consider financing you outside their area.

Vocational Courses

Discretionary. Many LEAs will not consider financing you outside their area unless the course you wish to do is *not* offered by their own colleges. The type of grant you are awarded may vary. Your LEA should be able to tell you the designation of your course and the type of award you might be eligible for.

Degree, DipHE and BTEC Higher Diplomas

Mandatory. Students are normally eligible for a major award.

Postgraduate Teacher Training Courses (ATC)(PGCE)

Students are normally eligible for an award from their LEA.

Postgraduate Courses – Higher Degrees, Diplomas, Certificates

For some courses of study you may qualify for a postgraduate bursary or studentship from the Department for Education and Employment. You should apply for nomination through your postgraduate college at the time you apply for the course. Otherwise, grants are awarded at the discretion of your LEA, or there may be scholarships awarded by the colleges to which you are applying. Some postgraduate courses will allow you to register as a part-time student, over a long period, and you will be able to support yourself with a part-time job. The course to which you are applying will tell you where you should seek finance.

Loans

Many would-be students for whom grants are not available are turning to student loans. Terms vary slightly but the deal is usually that you begin repayments to the Student Loans Company, normally by direct debit, in 60 instalments over five years, starting the April after you finish the course; payments can be deferred if you earn less than 85 per cent of the national average wage.

Repayment of government education grants usually begins three years after finishing further education; the repayment arrangements depend upon your earnings, and can be deferred if circumstances warrant.

Mature Students

It is not always necessary for mature entrants to have the minimum academic requirements for entry to courses, provided they can show they have the ability and creative potential to do the course. Some mature applicants may be required to do a test, or write an essay, in addition to attending an interview.

Some colleges may encourage mature applicants to acquire one or two GCSE or A levels or GNVQ equivalent in art and design or in other subjects before applying, particularly if they are in doubt about the applicants' motivation and ability to cope with the demands of the course if they have been outside full-time education for some time.

Chapter 5

Career Areas

Artists and designers go on to enter a wide variety of occupations after leaving college. Most art and design centres keep detailed information about the occupations entered by their students after college, and if you wish to find out more, you should contact individual departments or college careers advisers.

General Career Prospects

So what do art school-leavers do?

- □ They go on to *further study* in art and design, or further professional training, such as arts administration and art therapy, or apply to the various government enterprise programmes and allowance schemes as a potential small business.
- □ They enter one-year courses of *teacher training* as specialist art teachers in secondary schools or as primary school teachers.
- □ They find *temporary work*, often unrelated to art, while trying to establish themselves in *self-employment*, including freelancing, setting up a craft workshop, and consultancy.
- □ They enter *art and design-related jobs*, for example, an assistant art editor on a magazine, a ceramic designer in industry, a graphic designer in a design consultancy, a mural artist on an arts project, an art therapy assistant.
- □ They go into jobs where their *art and design background* is useful – such as in exhibition and museum work, advertising account executive, retail buying, arts administration.
- □ They enter *occupations open to all graduates*, regardless of subject – in retail management, administration, tourism and leisure, or even accountancy and computing.
- □ They travel abroad to broaden their experience.

In general, the more highly qualified you are, the more likely you are to find a job. The achievement of a degree or diploma in itself, together with other personal skills and interests, may combine to equip artists and designers for careers in many fields, both related and unrelated to their course of study. For many art students, the opportunity to spend three or four years at college may have been an end in itself, an important stage in their personal development.

What Are the Prospects?

Thanks, in part, to the economic successes of the early 1980s, the western world has become much more design conscious. This, in turn, meant more opportunities for designers, not only in industry proper, but the independent designers and craftspeople producing one-off and limited edition products were also enjoying a new recognition on this wave of design awareness. Artists and designers became the new celebrities; they became more visible and achieved more credibility in industry.

Manufacturers have learnt the importance of design, that design sells, and when you think of their sponsorship of the arts it is obvious that industry saw that art had cachet. Forward-thinking companies have realised the benefits of having designer/managers of production and sales people with design backgrounds. Thanks to schemes such as the Graduate Enterprise Programme and Business Start-up Support, it is possible for artists, designers and craftspeople to fund their own businesses.

While it would be misleading to say that employment prospects have improved for art and design graduates, the broadening of the range of jobs now available does present a more positive situation. However, jobs are no less competitive in a world where people are becoming better qualified.

Postgraduate Study

For many advanced courses it is often desirable and sometimes compulsory for applicants to have developed their work independently for at least one year after leaving art school. Funding for postgraduate study has diminished over the years, DFEE bursaries being the main source of support for higher degrees and diplomas in art and design. Increasingly, in response to the shortage of finance, many postgraduate centres now accept applicants on a part-time basis for higher degrees and advanced diploma courses (See Chapter 8.)

What Skills Do Artists/Designers Need to Survive After College?

First of all they should look at their own personal needs. Then at what skills and interests they have. What kind of lifestyle do they want – in the short term and in the long term? In addition they need to be:

- ☐ well-informed
- ☐ realistic
- ☐ self-motivated
- ☐ adaptable to change
- ☐ flexible
- ☐ persistent
- ☐ creative beyond their degree
- ☐ professional and able to see art in a wider context

Recreating a college environment, by establishing a network of friends and contacts, grouping together with others, sharing skills and experiences, and joining artists' and designers' organisations, can help to counter feelings of isolation after college. Most importantly, artists need to assess their skills and find ways of using these in other settings after college.

Creative and Performing Arts

Depending on their interests, graduates from these courses may be well equipped to enter postgraduate study in a specialised field, such as theatre management, arts administration, the visual arts, art history, or may go on to further professional training in dance, drama or music. Relevant occupations may include: teaching after a one-year postgraduate course; arts administration, in galleries, theatre, music, regional arts associations; in television, radio and film – as researchers, performers, designers, production assistants; in community arts, particularly where the course has a strong community element; youth and community work; work in magazine and book publishing;

journalism; in visual art and design; or work as performers in dance, drama or music.

Fashion and Textile Design

Generally speaking, fashion and textile design students hope to seek occupations related to their training. They may have studied from a range of options: fashion design, footwear design, carpet design, furnishing textiles, fashion textiles, embroidery, knitted and printed textiles, weaving, and so on. Some courses also include business administration elements which may lead to careers in management in the fashion and textile industries.

Fashion Design Studios

Many students specialising in fashion design or in textiles for fashion hope to find work as design assistants in the studios and work rooms of fashion companies from the well-known 'designer names' producing original collections (where few posts exist), right down to the popular end of the market where designs must be easily mass-produced interpretations of current trends.

The more mass-produced garments are, the more restrictions there can be on scope for the designer when available production methods, the choice of suitable fabrics, and the views of marketing and production staff all dictate to an extent the final appearance of a garment. A designer needs to be well informed, and may spend a considerable amount of time researching, visiting shows of fashion collections, talking to buyers and marketing staff, selecting suitable fabrics – and looking at the portfolios of students seeking jobs. Designs are not the products of pure inspiration. A combination of creative talent and an understanding and awareness of production and business problems is essential.

Case Study

Andrew left the Royal College of Art five years ago.

> 'I was always interested in fashion and left school at 16 to take a GAD National Diploma course with a fashion specialisation. At 18 I was accepted on to the BA (Hons) degree course at Nottingham Trent Polytechnic. I felt I needed more time to develop my work and made a successful application to the RCA.'

He won a number of national and international awards and competitions while a student, and also worked both freelance and on placement during vacations as designer and pattern cutter, the work varying between suppliers of mass market/high street stores in Britain and a high fashion designer label in Italy.

> 'On leaving the RCA at the age of 23, I was immediately offered a job in Germany working for an international fashion company. I turned this job down in favour of a job in England which offered broader experience working for a manufacturer supplying mass market multiples. The job involved fabric selection, liaising with buyers, creating and presenting theme boards, designing and personally cutting the selected designs, as well as overseeing the sample room production. Work was not seasonal and samples were produced continuously, with constant pressure always to include versions in the range of important and directional items seen on the international catwalks. From here I moved on to senior designer at Alexon International where my work was varied and challenging. I worked within a large team, and became responsible for designing day and evening dresses and soft suitings, as well as researching for all areas including tailoring and knitwear. The work involved compiling theme and mood boards for each season, selecting a colour palette, researching and liaising with both UK and international fabric agents as well as designing.
>
> 'After doing specific drawings for the sample room, I would then oversee the garments at toile stage, taking responsibility for the correct pads, buttons, zips, trims and so on. Finished garments were delivered to me before I presented them to my design executive.
>
> 'I was also heavily involved in pricing meetings, fittings and organising the finished range for the press shows and photographic shoots.'

A few years later, after moving on to other similar jobs and having completed several prestigious freelance commissions, Andrew decided the time was right to embark on a long-term dream to team up with an ex-colleague from his days at Nottingham: *Reynold.*

Reynold's career had followed similar lines: an MA at Central St Martin's led to a design job with John Galliano, other industrial experience and, again, exciting freelance commissions. With an enormous variety of experience under their belts they thought they would complement each other perfectly and formed the label Pierce Fionda. They used all their joint resources and charm to raise finance and negotiate good deals for showing and selling their collections with the right people, contacts made while in employment. They were an instant success – so much so that they had to close their order books. This was only part of it. They then had to get the clothes made to standard and delivered on time, and this is where their backgrounds really paid off.

They see their periods in employment as a kind of apprenticeship, learning far more than they ever realised. This knowledge and experience is helping to underpin their future which, judging from the success of their follow-up collections, is looking very rosy. In autumn 1995 they were chosen as 'New Generation Designers of the Year' by the British Fashion Council.

Fashion Illustration

This is an area where, traditionally, specific training has not existed. Most successful fashion illustrators trained as fashion designers by way of degree courses. Most people will confirm that, having gone through the rigours of conventional, design-based degree courses, the would-be illustrator not only has a rounded view of the whole industry and the illustrator's role within it, but also a sound understanding of garment construction, fabrics and the body. However, in response to the growing interest in this area, a number of colleges are now offering fashion illustration options. For more information, see *Careers in Fashion* (Kogan Page).

Case Study

Hilary followed a two-year Fine Art course at Ahmadu Bello University in Nigeria where her parents were then working. As this was recognised as a Foundation course, back in England she was able to enter the second year at Bradford College of Art, starting in textiles but changing mid-course to fashion, concentrating on drawing. She realised that she wanted to specialise in fashion illustration so, after qualifying, she took a one-year advanced course at Central St Martin's.

Her first job was with Nigel French (Forecast/Design Consultancy) where she stayed for ten years illustrating monthly retail reports, design forecasts, knitwear reports and special design projects for manufacturers in Australia, the USA, Canada, Japan and South Africa. The work involved regular visits to Paris, Milan, Florence and Rome to cover press shows, trade fairs and shops, gathering information, then illustrating after returning to

London. Having made quite a few contacts through small illustration jobs, mainly for *Drapers' Record* magazine, she eventually decided to become freelance and now operates from her home studio, working mainly for design consultancies and companies such as Marks and Spencer, Courtaulds, Burton Group and IWS, plus a small amount of magazine work. She continues to travel to European fashion centres and to New York fairly frequently for one or two of the smaller consultancies.

She enjoys the freedom of choosing her own hours of work but the tight deadlines and the chasing of clients for overdue payments can sometimes be very frustrating.

Hilary has also been invited to do occasional spells of teaching but is not so keen on that! She enjoys being freelance and working at home and doesn't miss the tedium of daily commuting.

Textile Designers

The textile industry in the UK is, sadly, on the decline because of the large amount of cheap imports from developing countries entering the market. Therefore, opportunities for textile designers with many of our large manufacturers are no longer available. However, some surviving textile manufacturers employ freelance designers, even if they do not actively recruit full-time staff. There has been a revival in the small design workshop, producing one-off or limited edition designs. Some textile designers work as designer/craftspeople, designing and producing their own work for exhibition, direct sale, or through limited retail craft outlets.

Textile design includes printed, knitted and woven textiles for garments, for household use, for furnishings or sometimes for decoration – as wall hangings, for example. There are ancillary areas, such as embroidery, lace and trimmings.

Case Studies

Sue completed a Foundation course near her home in the north west following through with a three year degree at Nottingham Trent University where she specialised in printed textiles. She then went on to complete a further one and a half year MA course at Birmingham (now the University of Central England). 'This enabled me to experiment further with printing techniques and design concepts suitable for both the fashion and furnishing industries.'

This in itself was unusual as textile designers usually specialise in one area or the other. Sue then moved to London where she worked for three different design studios, learning how to adapt her ideas for the commercial market, and about the different requirements of the printed textile industry around the world.

After four years' training in the industry (this is how she saw her employment), she felt she had enough experience to produce design collections independently and teamed up with a partner from a fashion background. They designed, manufactured and marketed their own collection for a couple of years before deciding to concentrate on 'the designs themselves' and allow larger manufacturers to concentrate on the production.

The print design studio is run from Sue's home in London. She herself designs and acts as an agent for 12 freelance designers in Australia, Europe, Scandinavia, and uses an additional agent to represent her studio in the USA and Japan.

The collection consists of one-off fashion prints suitable for all areas of the industry, eg menswear, dress, swimwear, sportswear and childrenswear. The turn-over of ideas is tremendous as each designer is constantly working on new techniques, print processes, colour combinations and imagery to make the collection innovative yet commercial.

> 'We work one and a half years ahead of what is seen in the shops. This allows the convertors to purchase prints, have the base cloths dyed and printed and available for the fashion designers to use for their collections.'

The 'team' has been carefully selected from the graduation shows over a five-year period to the collection.

> 'As we cater for such a diverse market we have to incorporate a real variety within the collection. I now feel the balance is just right between the creativity of designing and the excitement of selling these concepts all over the world.'

Sally and Kim trained as textile artists and started applying this to clothes. They designed a range of handpainted shirts and dresses. They started off getting orders by making appointments with fashionable shops, which led to a concession in a smart shop with branches in Bond Street and Hampstead. This worked well initially, but the shops went into liquidation and they were left with debts.

This setback prompted them to look into the possibility of selling their work directly to the public through a market stall at Covent Garden. They would recommend this method as an excellent way to start a business for the following reasons:

- □ You get.immediate feedback on your work and can increase production on popular lines, while still being able to experiment with new designs or follow trends.
- □ Cash flow: outgoings are kept low, and customer pay when items are sold rather than the credit that shops ask for.
- □ Prices are better. Shops mark up at least 117.5 per cent and often up to 300 per cent.

The business outgrew the stall and they sold to major retailers such as Paul Smith, Jones, Harvey Nichols and major stores in the USA.

Sally and Kim would urge caution as far as expenditure on trade shows are concerned; this expense, combined with bulk production costs, and the possible delays in payments from shops, affects cash flow and reduces profits.

They stopped working in the fashion business in 1988 after realising that for them, their homeware products were more rewarding and satisfying. They now run a successful furnishing fabric company.

Freelance Designers

On leaving college, some students successfully support themselves on a freelance basis working from home or in their own studios – possibly producing designs commissioned or bought by clothing manufacturers, or furnishing and fashion textiles manufacturers. Some manage to set up their own small businesses where they design and produce garments on a small scale and sell through their own shops, by mail order, or through a limited number of retail outlets.

Case Study

From school *Fifi* went to her local art school in West London to do a Foundation course where she realised her interests and strengths were in fashion and textiles. Knowing that ultimately she would want to work as a freelance designer, Fifi chose to study Fashion and Textile Design with Administration at Brighton University, a four-year sandwich course with one year working in industry. She spent her industrial year working for six months in a Yorkshire-based mill and six months at a knitwear design company in London.

> 'I found the experience of working in industry was invaluable to the extent that I recognised what I did and didn't want to do.
>
> 'After leaving college, my collection attracted a lot of attention from foreign retail buyers, leading to the problem of how and where to get small orders made up. Financing, producing, and marketing a collection by myself proved too demanding, so when I was offered a job with a high profile Parisian label I jumped at the chance to live and work in Paris.
>
> 'Working abroad, however, is not all as glamorous as it seems. I found myself feeling extremely isolated and lonely at times, although the work experience proved to be invaluable. I moved around a little, working full-time for a few people before going freelance. I worked on contracts for clients in France, the USA, Italy and Hong Kong.
>
> 'After six years in Paris I moved back to England and took a year and a half off, after which I took on the job which I continue to do now, working with a fashion design consultancy in London. My diverse work experience proved to be an advantage in my present job where our clients are varied.
>
> 'I have recently reduced my work at the consultancy to three days per week, moved to Brighton and commute. I spend the rest of the week developing freelance projects from my studio by the sea. I hope eventually to have my own collection and have it manufactured in the Far East.'

Fine Art

Fine art graduates do not necessarily expect to incorporate their fine art into future employment. 'I have no wish to include my art – except my artistic sense – in my work, and although it remains a very important part of my life, and I still practise, it remains a private thing,' says one ex-student. For many, the course may have been an end in itself.

But it is clear that some have set out from college with the aim of developing their work, possibly seeking commissions, selling work to galleries, and arranging individual and group shows of their work. After leaving college it may take, at the earliest, six months to complete sufficient new work in order to exhibit and to be successful in applying for grants and bursaries. There may be periods of unemployment or part-time and temporary work to achieve this end. The lack of studio space, college facilities and money with which to live and buy materials are often obstacles to be overcome, but a few who are determined do survive. (See Chapter 6.)

After college, fine artists enter a wide variety of occupations, often following a different job and pursuing their art at home.

Art teaching seems an obvious occupation, as a way of maintaining an involvement with work while earning a living, but in recent years job opportunities have declined.

A few enter 'graduate' occupations in management roles – in occupations which are regularly entered by graduates from other arts disciplines such as history, philosophy and languages. Others are known to obtain posts or seek further training in arts administration, museums and art galleries, community arts, art therapy, and in design areas – advertising, graphics and illustration, carpet and textile design, other product/industrial design, theatre design, scenic design in television, art restoration and conservation.

Graphic Design

After leaving college, graphic designers find work in design consultancies; advertising agencies; in magazine and book publishing; in television and film companies; with printers; with in-house design groups in industrial and commercial companies; in education; in museums, art galleries and arts organisations, local authorities and government departments. With the skills they have acquired at college, designers may specialise in graphic design, magazine design, packaging, photography, illustration, audio-visual materials, technical graphics, display and exhibition design, or typography. (A typographer is concerned with choosing the right typeface or lettering for a piece of artwork.) Of course, many designers will need skills in some or all of these areas in any one job.

Advertising Agencies

Advertising agencies are major employers of graphic designers. Their work may involve visualising ideas for packaging, television advertising, point-of-sale display and so on, and the designer will need to be competent in all graphic design skills, though in the larger advertising agencies specialists such as typographers and photographers may be employed. The designer must be able to work as a member of a team, often under pressure to meet deadlines. Advertising is a competitive world but promotion prospects are fairly good, as long as the ideas keep flowing and the artwork is of a high standard.

Case Study

Stephen, a graphics student, entered as a trainee art director with a large advertising agency where he learnt the basic art direction skills, technical skills, how advertising works, and also travelled abroad to visit other agencies. After a year he was offered a post of art director with another agency, and after a further six months moved to a larger agency. He felt that these frequent moves early in his career were natural for him, but others may stay longer in their first job.

> 'My job is art director. The job entails devising advertisements for press or television, and seeing them through to their printed or televised stage. After the idea is approved, a photographer or illustrator is hired (or a director for a commercial) by the art director to complete the artwork. Copy is set as briefed, and mechanicals (the finished artwork ready for reproduction) for print production made up. The art director oversees all these processes and is responsible for the finished look of the ad. This is a creatively satisfying job, and unlike some areas of the art world, money is not a problem when producing work. The job is also financially very rewarding. I intend to continue to gain experience as an art director and hope to do more television work in the future.'

Design Consultancies

Design consultancies are independent firms of designers employing several different kinds of designer: graphic, package, product, display, exhibition, textile, furniture, interior designers, and may undertake major and minor design jobs for industrial and commercial companies. For example, a new prestige bookshop is opening shortly. The owner brings in the design consultancy to design the shop interior, all point-of-sale display fittings and all business stationery to be used – from sale wrapping paper to company invoices and sales slips. When the shop is due to open, the design team works on the promotion and publicity material and press advertisements. Some design studios and consultancies, however, may be more specialised in their approach, offering, for example, purely graphic design and publicity services. Colin, a graphic designer, said, 'I find working in a design consultancy extremely stimulating. There is such a cross-fertilisation of ideas, with so many different designers working together and the scope of work can be so varied. One day I might be designing simple letterheads. Another, I might be the member of a design team looking at the problems associated with an international company wishing to update its image – its advertising materials, its stationery, the layout and interior of its premises and so on ...'

Addresses of design consultancies and of professional designers are maintained by the Chartered Society of Designers which also runs a staff vacancy service. A register of designers' services appears every month in *Design* magazine.

Publishing

Book publishers and magazine publishing houses, or those concerned with the production of both books and magazines, employ graphic designers as art assistants and art directors. The art director or designer is responsible for the overall visual appearance of the book or magazine which he/she carries out in consultation with the editorial staff. This may involve choosing appropriate typefaces, deciding on the layout of pages or book covers, and the overall design, often employing the services of freelance illustrators and photographers for the necessary visual extras.

Case Study

At 18 *Nicky* completed a BTEC National Diploma in General Art and Design, with a strong portfolio in drawing and, having gained an introduction to a range of art and design disciplines, she chose to pursue a degree course in Visual Communication at Bath, (now Graphic Design BA Hons). She was sure at once that this suited her.

> 'The course had a varied and exciting first year with drawing, graphic design, animation, time-based media, photography and illustration. I was encouraged to explore my potential in all these areas and could choose either a multi-option final year or a more specific route.

'My continuing fascination with drawing led me towards illustration and on completion of my degree I was accepted on a year's honorary postgraduate fellowship in Printmaking and Papermaking. This was structured by myself with the use of workshops and a free studio. The following summer I taught Papermaking at a summer school in France.

'After four years studying in Bath I moved to London to start a part-time postgraduate course in illustration at Central St Martin's. This offered advice from working illustrators, "live projects" and a place to discuss ideas and learn more about the business of illustration. I started working freelance. After a couple of years, I realised the isolated lifestyle of an illustrator did not suit me, coupled with a hard financial struggle within a depressed economic climate. I decided to try other avenues of design and started working for a photographer's agent and had ideas about becoming an art buyer in an advertising agency. Unexpected redundancy led me to question my choice and I worked part-time as a mural painter and as a photographer's stylist.

'With a life-long interest in books I started working part-time as a traditional paste-up artist for a small press – Redstone Press – producing art books and a diary each year. My work covered researcher and traditional paste-up artist.

'After this apprenticeship I wanted to become more involved in the design process and applied to work at Dorling Kindersley – a large, international publishers renowned for its Eye-Witness children's series of books and its innovative use of photography and illustration. I learnt a lot during this period, working closely with the author as part of a team of designers and editors, working to a budget and schedule, researching and collating information from outside organisations for image reference, liaising with picture researchers, ordering and selecting transparencies. I designed spreads from initial ideas to final layouts and ready to print, visualising artworks, models and photography. The book could also involve art directing shoots and buying props. Designers have to keep to production deadlines, liaising with the production department and colour correcting proofs. I learnt to use Quark Xpress and other Mac programs, a skill that had eluded me until this point!

'After completing a number of books I saw a job teaching graphic design part-time on a Foundation course. I was looking for a new challenge and change of direction. It was an opportunity to return some of my knowledge to education and I enjoy the intellectual stimulation and the diversity of my job.

'I am currently working on a monthly magazine as part of a job share. This is as a designer producing spreads from ideas to print with very strict production deadlines. The work is varied and the day rate higher than in publishing. It is a change to work at a much faster pace although the final product is eventually thrown away which I do not find very satisfying.

'I spend the rest of the week working in my studio at home on an idea for a book which I intend to present to publishing houses when it is at a more complete stage. Time to do my own work is an important part of my working week.

'Interesting work and having a satisfying and creative life are my motivating factors, huge financial rewards have never been a goal. Working freelance enables me to change my work direction or combine a variety of jobs in the art and design field.'

Freelance Designers

Few graphic designers attempt full-time freelance work or set up their own design studios immediately on leaving college, though after only one or two years in employment they may well do so, when they have sufficient commercial experience to be able to understand and interpret the needs of the clients, organise and run their own business and set up their own studio. The section on freelance illustration (p 56) has many points in common with the work of the freelance designer (see Chapter 6).

Graphic Designers in Television

The work of the graphics department in a television company is extremely wide-ranging. It includes typography, lettering, doing simple credits and captions, designing mobiles, weather charts, cartoons and animation, designing lettering and a presentation style for a series or special programme, making props such as charts, and even passports, foreign money, ration books, and other historical and period props. Graphic designers often regard themselves as experts in producing authentic material, as well as original designs. All designers are art college trained, with degrees or diplomas in graphic design. Most illustration work is carried out by freelance illustrators who are used on a regular basis, though some illustrators have been recruited in full-time posts to do both illustration and design. Increasingly, the computer is being used in television graphics. The future application of modern technology in this field will require designers to be more flexible in their skills. Art and design college-leavers with or without some work experience may be recruited as assistant designers.

Further information about career prospects, salaries, and

other kinds of work undertaken by designers may be obtained from the BBC and ITV companies, and you may find it helpful to contact the senior designer or the recruitment department at your local TV station.

Technical Graphic Artists

Those who wish to enter more technical work may find employment in industrial companies, often allied to the engineering industry, and in other fields such as building, architecture, scientific and biological work, and in medical work. In the engineering field the work may involve preparing drawings and plans from written specifications. This requires good interpretation skills in converting figures to two- and three-dimensional drawings in an accurate way. Work in these areas is being revolutionised by developments in computer illustration and computer-enhanced illustration.

Case Study

Andy trained as a graphic designer but decided to enter the technical field. He works for a technical instrument company, mostly working on plans and drawings with research and development engineers who are designing new components. He also helps with training aids and produces some audio-visual material using design and photographic skills. He finds the job pays well and gives him the variety he needs. The level of accuracy and professionalism required in producing finished engineering drawings is to him the most challenging and satisfying part of the job. Increasingly, computer graphics is being introduced, especially in these technical areas. Some design consultancies may also employ technical graphic artists and illustrators.

Other Areas of Employment

Most educational establishments, such as universities and the Open University, have media or educational technology departments employing technicians and sometimes graphic designers. Commercial and industrial companies may have in-house design groups. Public relations departments in local authorities sometimes employ designers. Exhibition organisers and consultants employ interior, exhibition and graphic designers; many employ freelances, often having a 'portfolio' of designers whom they can call upon for specific work. Printing firms may employ typographers and graphic designers.

Case Study

Rob is a designer/junior art director with a record company.

> 'I got the job because the art director remembered me from a visit I had made eight months previously while still at college. I work with fairly strict budgets, and usually in close conjunction with the "artistes". Designs and artwork must be produced to package and promote the music produced (the product). This involves finding the right visual imagery to fit the music and the optimum method of producing the design decided upon, ie choosing and commissioning the illustrator or photographer where necessary. The actual design work I do myself wherever possible. There is satisfaction in seeing a job through from initial concept to finished product and of course (it would be foolish to pretend otherwise) to find out other people's reactions to how successfully the record is finally packaged. It is challenging to have to inform, advertise, help to make the product desirable, and yet still retain a closeness with the music and not affect the credibility of the performer.'

Some record companies will employ their own designers; others will use the services of freelance staff or advertising and publicity agencies. The music press and the *Music Yearbook* are helpful for ideas and addresses.

Illustration

Illustrators emerging from specialist illustration and graphic design courses may find full-time employment as designers/illustrators, but more often are commissioned by magazine and book publishers, design consultancies, advertising agencies and other employers on a freelance basis, sometimes through an artists' agent. Illustrators may also receive commissions by exhibiting work through galleries. In addition, scientific and technical illustrators may find freelance work, and sometimes full-time employment, in industry, medical and scientific publishers, research establishments, government departments, the National Health Service and in museums.

Case Study

Marty came through what she calls 'the usual school route': O level art, A level art. She always wanted to draw so she enrolled on a one-year Foundation course at Sheffield Poly.

> 'It was a really fab start, opening my eyes to the range of options including fine art, sculpture, silversmithing and graphic design. If the college at Sheffield had done a graphics course I'd have stayed there to do a BA, but they didn't so I had to choose where and what to do. I still wanted to draw, but didn't know what!
>
> 'My tutor asked what I enjoyed doodling and I said "people figures", so he suggested fashion design. Perplexing. Then we had a big meeting where we all had to say what course we'd chosen, so I decided fashion there and then, without actually looking into it at all.'

From 1974 to 1977 Marty studied BA Hons Fashion Design at Manchester Polytechnic. She always wanted to do more drawing and found the course a struggle; at the end of the first year she almost switched to Fine Art. She hated the emphasis on pattern cutting and couldn't see it as creative. In the second year, under the influence of visiting lecturer Victor Herbert, she felt inspired and was encouraged, 'His emphasis suited me particularly well – drawing, and tons of it!'

As a consequence, her final year was a great success and she had a strong portfolio with an emphasis on illustration.

> 'After the degree show I went to London to look for work in design or illustration. I'd been advised not to expect a full-time job in fashion illustration initially, so, I did the rounds of junior designer interviews.' One day, she decided to pursue another tack and took her portfolio to Indesign, asking specifically about illustration.
>
> 'They were encouraging, but no actual work came up, so I continued to show my work to anyone who'd look. Wendy Dagworthy (then very much the young designer of the moment) was very helpful and suggested DHI. Others were helpful too; at this point I was pestering for advice rather than work.
>
> 'I literally camped out at DHI until someone was available to see me and my folio! I was right to be persistent and fortunately they took the gamble and gave me a three-month probationary contract (on a full-time/freelance basis) to illustrate first childrenswear then womenswear and later menswear. What a rookie I was. Still am: it's a long learning curve!
>
> 'DHI was great. The whole experience was of learning, very valuable. I worked there for five years.'

When she decided to work freelance, she had acquired good contacts for fashion illustration through full-time work. But,

> 'I'd always wanted to do general illustration so I began a folio of more varied work. This still continues. Self-promotion is important; it's not only cheap but is also essential once you've established a working style, gained experience on magazines, etc. It's important that your work is seen by art buyers. I take a page in an art annual each year, which is read by people I wouldn't get to see. It's time-consuming to organise to see every overworked art director in the industry, although it is good to do so in the early days when you're becoming established.
>
> 'Being reliable, professional, consistent and available to work are vital qualities. I found it necessary to build a relationship of trust with clients, who may become regulars now or in the future.
>
> 'When presenting yourself and your folio, all the commonsense rules apply, but I always kept a fairly small selection of art work – well edited, as I found that art editors' time is precious too.
>
> 'From the art annuals I was approached by artists' agents. I was wary for a while as I was getting enough work by myself. But it can be a mutually beneficial experience if you're willing to work with your agent to make progress and continue to self-promote. It changed the way I worked and saw my work.
>
> 'I get editorial/publishing work by having colour postcards printed of a recent piece of work and mailing them to magazines, etc. My agent deals with advertising only. Fees for advertising work can be good but it's not regular: famine or feast! The backing of a good agent can be valuable but there are no guarantees of work, so I keep an eye on things I should be doing to generate work.
>
> 'Sometime I feel I'll never get used to the ups and downs of freelance, but it's true that you get out what you put into work and I love illustrating!'

Who Can Help You to Get Started?

Staff at college, past students and established illustrators may be able to advise on practical issues, as will potential employers such as art directors with publishing companies and advertising agencies. The Association of Illustrators is the professional body. It is concerned with all aspects of illustrating, provides advisory services and promotes illustrators' work. It also organises an annual exhibition of illustrators, and publications include a regular newsletter and a *Survival Kit* which is particularly useful for the newly qualified illustrator. The kit covers all aspects of the work of the freelance illustrator, from setting up a studio and how to promote yourself, to what clients expect of illustrators, and useful reference sections on courses, printing jargon, and a list of artists' agents and their services.

How to Begin Finding Work

Some illustrators apply for design jobs initially to gain some work experience and make contacts before taking on full-time freelance work. Some may take temporary work or a part-time job while building up their freelance work; others may have already begun freelancing before leaving college and find that their work increases steadily from these initial contacts. The degree or diploma show at the end of the course brings many visitors to art and design departments, such as art directors from advertising agencies and publishing houses and artists' agents, all looking for new talent. Many illustrators find their first commissions in this way.

Making direct approaches to art directors with publishers, advertising agencies, design studios, television, or to artists' agents can be a daunting prospect. But art directors, on the whole, are keen to meet new college-leavers and see their work. This involves assembling a portfolio of your work and fixing up visits by letter or telephone. This is the advice of one illustrator; 'Do your homework first. Find out what publications/type of books/publicity styles are produced by the organisation you are approaching. Take a good selection of work – finished artwork and working drawings, but not too much. Whoever you will see will have opinions about your work. Make sure you have your own opinions and don't be prepared to compromise on your work for the sake of getting a commission. If you're good enough, an art director somewhere will appreciate your style of work and be able to use you – if not now, possibly at a later date.' Sometimes, art directors may be able to advise you and recommend you to others – you need to be persistent in making contacts. One illustrator said she contacted 30 publishers in two months.

Artists' agents act on behalf of illustrators, finding them work with advertising agencies, publishing houses and so on. Agents often charge a hefty commission (25 per cent upwards), but many illustrators use them, so you then don't have to spend valuable time looking for work.

Working With Other Illustrators

Some illustrators find it easier to work in groups, and may collectively be able to afford rent for a studio. Working together prevents feelings of isolation and loneliness; there are other people with whom to bounce ideas around; contacts made by individuals may benefit the group as a whole. However, the success of a group studio depends very much on the individuals involved, and you must decide whether this mode of working really does suit you – or whether you would find it too distracting or disrupting.

Case Study

Jon took a slightly different route into illustration from most artists: after leaving school with O and A levels he completed a Foundation course and went on to study Graphic Design at Central St Martin's; it was not until the beginning of his third year that he changed to specialise in illustration.

> 'I was advised to take an extra year to fully develop an illustrative style.
>
> 'This route has been a great advantage for me; studying graphics gave me a full understanding of the graphic design world from placements as an art director in an advertising agency and a design group. It also gave me a confidence and great love of typography.
>
> 'Central St Martin's prepared me extremely well for life as a professional illustrator; all the tutors were practising illustrators and we had regular projects with art directors.
>
> 'Some people got a lot of contacts from their degree show; I got one commission but the majority of my work came from interviews I organised with art directors. In my first year as a graduate I went on the Enterprise Allowance Scheme, which was invaluable for establishing my career, allowing me to concentrate on building a folio of commissioned work and not worrying about money.
>
> 'I have been working full-time as a freelance illustrator/photographer since graduating in 1989. I started by producing flat and slight relief collage illustrations and gradually moved into producing 3D illustrations and photography, then on to 5 x 4 transparencies. I still enjoy it greatly and have lots of ideas on how my work can develop.
>
> 'The last few years have been very busy. I have worked for a wide range of clients from magazines, design companies, advertising agencies to cable television. In 1994 I started advertising in the illustrators' book, *Contact*, the directory most widely used by art directors to commission work. It has brought in a lot of work. I was

also approached by an agent who now represents me, although I still get work outside the agency.

'It is a profession that suits me really well as I have control of my work environment and to some extent decide when I work. It's extremely rewarding running your own business. I work from home, rather than a studio which I might find distracting. One week I'll be working on a magazine illustration, the next a brochure cover, the next an animated sequence.

'To be an illustrator you need to have a lot of get up and go and be able to pick yourself up from a knock-back. You must also have a lot of self-discipline, self-motivation and have good time management, along with the ability to get on with a wide range of people, and lots of enthusiasm.'

History of Art

Graduates in the history of art and the history of design may enter further study and occupations related or unrelated to their degree subject.

- □ Postgraduate academic study or research in art history, design history, etc at universities. Some have followed study or training in other areas, such as arts administration, librarianship, secretarial work, the Works of Art course at Sotheby's, and even in fine art or restoration – if students are sufficiently competent in the practice of artwork. (A number of art history students continue with their artwork while studying for their degree, although it may not be part of the course.)
- □ Teacher training – although few art history specialist teachers are employed in secondary education, it may be combined with other subjects or within general studies for the purposes of training and obtaining a teaching post later. There are few posts in further and higher education, many of which are more often taken up by those who have completed a higher degree.
- □ Employment – history of art degrees may be relevant in occupations such as work in museums and art galleries; arts administration; with art publishers as researchers, copywriters, production assistants; restoration – if the practice of artwork is up to standard. They may also enter graduate occupations in industry, commerce, and local and central government.

Three-Dimensional Design

(including industrial design, product design, interior design, theatre design)

Three-dimensional design students from all subjects may go on to postgraduate study in a specialist area: jewellery, industrial design, furniture, ceramics, theatre design. Some may enter teacher training where there is a shortage of teachers in craft, design and technology skills, though students of three-dimensional subjects may also be found teaching visual arts subjects.

Many degree and vocational courses offer ceramics, furniture, jewellery, silversmithing, wood, metals, glass and plastics – where the design of functional or decorative objects may be the chief activity of the course. Some leavers may prefer to work as artists/craftspeople or designers, producing one-off objects in their own workshops, whereas others may apply their skills to more commercially orientated design, working on designs to be produced on a larger scale by manufacturing industry. Work as an artist or designer-craftsperson is described more fully in Chapter 6.

Industrial and Product Design

Think of any gadget or piece of equipment you use in everyday life: a bicycle, a car, a refrigerator, kitchen equipment, furniture, heaters; or something in working life: a typewriter, office equipment, computer terminals, medical equipment. Somewhere along the line, an industrial or product designer will have contributed to the finished article. Nowadays, most industrial or product designers have completed courses in three-dimensional, product or industrial design, though graphics and textiles designers and fine artists have also been known to enter this field. Industrial or product designers may be employed in design consultancies offering a range of design services to manufacturing and commercial companies, with in-house design groups in manufacturing industry, though some designers prefer to work freelance and build their own prototypes, with the aim of persuading a manufacturer to produce their designs on a commercial basis, or receive commissioned work. Some designers manufacture their own designs, where the production methods and equipment are on a small scale.

The work of the industrial designer has tremendous scope, but it should not be confused with that of the design engineer whose training will have been in engineering subjects and whose concern is the design of the mechanical, electrical or electronic function, rather than the appearance. At a show of postgraduate designers' work at the Royal College of Art, there were designs for baby slings, desktop computer housing, vacuum flasks, watches, kitchenware, seating and equipment for the handicapped – a 'hoverchair' and a braille self-tutor. The contribution of the designer to our living and working environment is something that is increasingly being recognised and valued by manufacturers and consumers alike.

The Design Council promotes the work of British designers in all fields, including and especially in industrial and product design. It cultivates good relationships with manufacturers, maintains a register of recognised designers, displays work in its gallery in London, and publishes a monthly journal, *Design*, which features new work by designers. Similarly, the Chartered Society of Designers, the designers' professional organisation, does much to improve standards of professionalism and promote the work of designers.

The work of the designer is chiefly concerned with the general aesthetic appearance of the product, but also must take into account the users' needs, and the manufacturing requirements. The designer may work closely with engineers and with production staff. Any small change in a design can mean changes in tooling-up for production. With strict budgets to work to, and possible production factors to take into account, the professional designer must consider the implications of his design work. At the end of the day, the product must look good, function well, and meet the users' needs. Some industrial design courses may include the study and application of engineering principles, whereas other three-dimensional design courses devote more time to creative elements.

Case Studies

Mike is a student of three-dimensional design working in the electrical industry, designing panels and 'cabinets' for cookers.

> 'In my designs, it's no good making changes without consulting the design engineer. Moving knobs and switches about to give a more streamlined appearance may create havoc with the wiring, and the cooker may not function so well. I need to have a basic sympathy for

engineering principles. I think taking cars to bits in my spare time while a student taught me a lot and gave me a good grounding for this job! I begin my designs and scale drawings, including colour schemes, and then move on to set up mock-ups and models for the panels. The design is taken further when we build it into prototype later on. All along the way I am consulting with the design engineers and other staff.'

Sue studied three-dimensional design with a product design bias, specialising in ceramics. She had some vacation work experience in the ceramics industry before graduating. Her first job is as a design assistant in the design studio of a pottery firm, and her work is confined to surface decoration of tableware. The first few months in her job were spent learning about the whole industrial process, seeing each manufacturing stage and learning something of the technical and chemical processes involved. At present she is working on a theme for a new range of tableware in the mid-price range, under the supervision of a senior designer.

Jane specialised in furniture design, and since leaving college she has been employed as a designer with a company which markets office furniture and provides an office planning design service to their clients.

'My work entails space-planning offices using office furniture provided by the companies we represent. This involves technical drawings, plans, elevations, visuals, drawing up quotes for furniture for client presentation. I may be involved in developing furniture products to meet changes in demand of customer and market. I supervise installations of furniture, co-ordinate warehouse and stock control. I also produce visuals/technical drawings for brochures and advertising material, together with audio-visual drawings. This is a small firm, and in all, my work is very varied. The client liaison aspect is very important. As the work of the company develops, I hope I shall have opportunities for promotion. In my spare time I am studying for a Diploma in Marketing with the intention of learning business procedure/strategy/managerial considerations and markets . . .'

Ellen is an assistant goldsmith and designer with a firm of retail jewellers with its own workshop on the premises. She combines design and production work.

'I work under a younger and more skilled trade-trained goldsmith. I was lucky to find this job. After leaving my industrial design course (silversmithing) I had several temporary jobs before coming across this one. At present, my final degree show work is displayed in the jeweller's shop window, which I hope will be good for my future as a designer! I was taken on because the shop was running behind with orders – we take individual commissions, remodelling, etc, the only shop in the area to do so, and despite great uncertainty in the trade it seems to be thriving. Now, having learned not to "do everything backwards", I am trusted to do most of the simpler jobs and repairs that the menders won't do or have done wrong. It is most gratifying to find that you can do things, even if at first they are only very simple, to a very high standard and professional finish.'

Interior Design

Interior designers may join design practices – working with other interior designers and also with architects. Some may work in design practices and consultancies, offering a wider range of services alongside graphic designers, product designers, and textile designers. Other interior designers set up in freelance practice, though this is more likely after several years' experience in professional practice.

Interior designers may also join office furniture and design services, or work with in-house design groups, for example with furniture manufacturers, in the retail industry – providing bathroom and kitchen planning services to customers in the furniture department of a large store, or with hotel groups, building companies, and in some industrial companies. The interior designer has an important contribution to make to our living and working environment. Most interior design work is for industry, shop interiors and display, exhibitions, office interiors, hotels, businesses, airports, public buildings, and so on. Some interior designers may apply their design skills in other fields, such as theatre design, television set design, product design and so on.

Theatre Design

Many students of theatre and design hope to find work in occupations related to their studies: in theatre, dance, opera, film, television, chiefly as set and costume designers, and sometimes in technical areas such as lighting, or in more administrative roles, for example, in stage management. Theatre designers may work on a freelance basis, or be employed full-time by national or provincial performing companies, and in film and television. It is the job of the theatre designer to work closely with producers, directors and actors to create the right setting and overall visual effect for a production, whether it is a historical drama or a modern dance performance. This involves time spent in researching for themes and ideas. A sympathy for the performed work, and for the way in which it is interpreted by the actors and directors, is vital. In larger companies, set and costume design may be carried out by separate specialists, although with smaller companies the designer may be responsible for the design of properties and costume.

A set designer may begin work for a production by preparing scale drawings and models of sets to suggest an overall theme, colour and style. The work will also include the selection of properties and supervising the making of some special properties, scene painting and the general construction of sets. The completion of the work requires the ability to see through the visual ideas into constructed full-size sets, often on limited budgets and the supervision of craftspeople and scene painters. On leaving college, many newly qualified theatre designers begin work as assistants with small repertory companies, often in support roles, painting scenery, making costumes, or in community theatre. Others may be lucky to find design assistant posts with national theatre, opera and dance companies, or in film and television.

Case Studies

Roz, a theatre graduate, works on a freelance basis and found she had enough contacts who would give her work, mostly with small theatre companies which often cannot afford to take on full-time design staff.

> 'When I'm in work I seem to work 24 hours a day designing, making costumes and scene painting. When I'm out of work, I try to find out more, read, walk, visit companies. I am gradually building up contacts and hope to become a specialist in design for dance.'

Di is a milliner/jeweller with a large national theatre company. She wrote 'on spec' for the job and they asked her to come for interview. She works with one other colleague and it is their job to make all the hats for the main house shows.

'We work from designs and working drawings produced by senior designers. We are fortunate to work with leading international designers, from whom we learn a great deal. We also make a large amount of jewellery for production, often to our own design ideas, which I find very satisfying. During production we work lots of overtime, including weekends, but usually not later than 11 pm. Sometimes we can put our own designs into practice, after being given a rough idea of what is needed. My future plans are to find similar work with another large national company, maybe opera, to broaden my experience.'

Chapter 6

The Practising Artist, Craftsperson and Freelance Designer

Ways of Getting Established

Postgraduate study. This is a way of extending college life for up to three years, giving you the opportunity and facilities to carry on developing your work. During the course, many postgraduate students take on freelance work, have exhibitions and shows, and generally make good contacts vital to their future survival. An increasing number of postgraduate centres offer part-time study, or courses designed to help new craftspeople and designers to become established.

Further training. For artist-craftspeople – weavers, ceramic artists, silversmiths, those working in wood, metal or glass, and so on – wishing to set up their own studios, workshop experience may prove valuable. Art school-leavers can now apply to the various enterprise programmes sponsored by government funding. All offer a weekly income for one year, expect you to have at least £1,000 in cash or in kind (equipment) to invest in your business and have no other employment while receiving the allowance – working full-time at your business. These are: the Graduate Enterprise Programme, for business training and support while setting up your business; the Design Enterprise Programme, geared to the needs of designers and run by the London Enterprise Agency, and the Business Start-up scheme. Craftspeople setting up their first craft workshop business who are eligible for both the Business Start-up and the Crafts Council Setting Up Scheme may apply for both grants, provided they inform the Crafts Council at the time of application for the grant.

Other ways are to persuade craftspeople to take you on as an assistant for a small wage. A few specialised courses and training centres (for example, the John Makepeace School for Craftsmen in Wood, and the course for craftspeople at Chester College) offer a combination of professional study and workshop practice.

Employment. So what about a job? Designers may take full-time design jobs in order to gain professional experience before starting up on their own. Others may choose to take a part-time or temporary job of any kind, just to have a regular income, while continuing with their artwork as a main activity in their free time. Part-time teaching in an art school is often considered to be a good way of combining a job with personal work. However, these posts are more likely to go to established artists, designers and craftspeople or those from postgraduate courses.

One fine artist has found a job which suits his needs: 'I knew before starting the course that it was highly unlikely I would make a living at fine art. For nearly a year now I have been fully employed as a milkman. As this work involves early rising, it also finishes quite early, 4 am to 8.30 am (except on cash collecting days). This leaves me a lot of free time to paint, and the wages being reasonable for a six-day week supply ample finances. The job also gives me plenty of time to visit exhibitions in London ...'

Grants. The enterprise schemes mentioned on p 68 are providing much needed support for new college-leavers. Apart from this, the two main grant-awarding bodies for artists and makers are the Arts Council and the Crafts Council respectively. In conjunction with Regional Arts Boards they provide finance and assistance to the creative arts and crafts. For the new art college-leaver, there are few grants available. Most will require evidence of continuing development as an artist or craftsperson: recent exhibitions or shows, a collection of work *other than* that produced for a final degree or college diploma shows.

The Arts Council supports the creative arts in the following areas: painting, sculpture, printmaking, photography, film, community arts, literature, theatre, music and dance. The Crafts Council promotes and supports the work of craftspeople in ceramics, wood, furniture, glass, metal, textiles, bookbinding, and so on. Setting Up grants are available to makers who are within two years of setting up a business and whose work meets the criteria. Details of grants schemes may be obtained direct from the Arts and Crafts Councils or from Regional Arts Boards (see addresses on p 121).

Some independent charities, such as the Prince's Trust, industrial companies, colleges, schools and foundations support the arts by making awards to artists and designers in the form of competitions, grants, sponsored shows and exhibitions, commissioning works, travel scholarships, fellowships and bursaries. Most of these are advertised in the national press and in the specialist art journals (see p 126).

Where Will You Work?

Working at home can be ideal if you have the basic facilities you need, but it can be difficult to separate work from non-work and you may feel isolated. Many art school-leavers miss the facilities they had at college and have trouble finding a substitute. It may be impractical to work at home for other reasons – for example, if you are a sculptor and your work is on a large scale.

For those hoping for studio or workshop space, or needing access to expensive equipment and facilities such as a kiln, photographic studio or printmaking facilities, joining an existing workshop or studio can be the answer. Regional Arts Boards have addresses of artists and craftspeople, group workshops and studios and shared facilities in your area. If none exists, you may have to establish your own or join with a group of like-minded people to find premises. There are grants available to help artists and craftspeople establish new workshops, as has already been mentioned. Two other organisations, Acme Artists Housing Association and Space, which help artists acquire studio premises at reasonable rents in London, can also offer advice on all aspects of finding property, including tenancy agreements and leases to individuals and groups in other areas of the country. Freelance designers may be in a better position financially to rent studio premises as individuals or in a group on a commercial basis, possibly through estate agents. Some schemes exist whereby warehouses or large premises have been divided up into small rentable units, which suit the needs of small businesses, including the individual designer or a small group. Two examples are the Clerkenwell Workshops and the Barley Mow Workspace in London, and there are some in other parts of the country. Often commercial premises offered through estate agents are too expensive, particularly for the impoverished artist or craftsperson.

What other sources are there? Local authorities may be sympathetic and offer disused council property at a low rent, especially if it has a short life and may be demolished in a few years' time. Some local authorities and new town development corporations have made special provision for workshop and studio space available for practising artists and craftspeople. You may find some workspace through friends and acquaintances, but often one of the best ways is to look around locally for disused property such as in basements, top floors of warehouses, rooms above shops – and find out who owns them. You may be able to negotiate a fairly cheap rent with the landlord.

Legal and Financial Problems

Once you start setting up on your own you may encounter a number of financial and legal problems which, if ignored, will not go away; for example, tenancy agreements, contracts with galleries, submitting tax returns, keeping accounts, copyright, and so on. The *Artist's Newsletter* has published supplements on the Artist and Insurance, Copyright, National Insurance, Artists and Galleries, and other legal matters. The Chartered Society of Designers can help designers with professional queries. The Crafts Council also produces *Running a Workshop* (see p 127).

What Outlets are There for Your Work?

Establishing outlets for your work can begin at college. Many students have already begun freelance work, received commissions, have exhibitions arranged with galleries, or buyers for their work before leaving. They may make contacts through lecturing staff, through entering competitions, or from approaches made by visiting gallery owners, art directors, or buyers attending their final degree or diploma shows.

Once you have left college it may take some time before sufficient new work is completed. Time taken finding outlets is time away from your artwork; it is unlikely that people will come to your studio or workshop unless you are extremely lucky and have good contacts, or if you happen to operate a workshop/studio and gallery combined. Most people rely on galleries and other outlets to sell their work for them. Public and private galleries may not be the only places to give you a show. Try art festivals, arts centres, craft centres, arts and craft shops and galleries, small galleries-cum-workshops, bookshops, schools and colleges, and even banks, building societies, hotels and other commercial companies which may be pleased to show your work in their place of business.

Some artists and craftspeople feel they will never be able to produce enough work for a first show. Joining with others may help solve this – groups can often get exhibition space more easily than individuals, even if their artwork is fairly diverse. In contacting galleries or shops, it is best to write or phone beforehand for an appointment, to take along some slides or photographs, or examples of your work, and have some idea of what you want from them.

Once you begin to find outlets you should ask yourself: 'Can I produce the work on time? How do I cost and price my work? Does the gallery take a commission? Should my work be insured? Who will pay for the private view? Who will pay for the publicity? (and if you are selling work to a craft gallery), Have I costed out my time and materials so that I know what price to ask for my work? Am I sending work to the gallery on a sale-or-return basis? When will I be paid? Can I recall work for an exhibition? To answer these you can enlist the help of other artists or gallery owners to a certain extent, and follow up the helpful organisations listed on p 122 onwards. The Crafts Council maintains a list of craft galleries and shops. Galleries in the UK generally are listed in the *Arts Review Yearbook and Directory*. Other ways of publicising yourself include: Regional Arts Boards, which maintain registers of selected artists and craftspeople and keep slides of their work; the Crafts Council itself has an Index of Selected Makers and a National Register of Makers; Crafts Guilds also promote the work of the craftsperson.

Freelance designers, whether in textiles, graphics, production, or whatever, can publicise themselves through advertising in the local press or in selected journals, and through entries in directories such as *The Creative Handbook*. They may find work as a result of interest shown at their college degree or diploma shows, and through making contacts themselves and visiting potential clients with a portfolio of work. Further publicity may be achieved through acceptance and inclusion on the Design Council or Chartered Society of Designers' designer register.

Making a Living?

Very few artists and craftspeople are able to make a full-time living, particularly in the early stages. Many continue to supplement their work with full-time or part-time work, or with commercial freelance design work.

Case Studies

Fine artist:

> 'I have been able to carry on with my own work in a small way at the weekends and in the evenings. However, it has not been the production of artefacts that has been as important as extending my knowledge about art. The travelling that I did last year has been of great advantage to me. A year after graduation I had an exhibition of paintings and prints at a provincial art gallery. After the finals show I thought it would be good to work for another exhibition in a place more accessible to the public. It was well reviewed on Northern TV and in the press.'

Ceramics artist:

> 'When I left college, I was lucky – a friend offered me a room free of charge to work in. At my college degree show I was offered an exhibition in a London gallery. I set up my studio initially with a bank loan (though I'm still overdrawn). Almost a year after leaving I was successful in receiving an award from my Regional Arts Board towards workshop equipment. This year I have had two more shows in galleries. I have received many private commissions and am just about surviving, though I hope to get some part-time teaching in an art college next year. I enjoy the satisfaction of being 100 per cent creative every day, though I long for intellectual stimulus. I can be very lonely at times and I hope in the future to set up a studio with at least one other person to avoid being cut off. Up until recently I supplemented my income waitressing three nights a week, and I've also had to live on social security, declaring my earnings as they come in ...'

A small jewellery design business: Nick and Pat are jewellery designers who live and work in premises which combine a shop/ gallery in Brighton. On leaving college they worked for a dress designer, and in their spare time Nick painted and Pat designed and made clothes which they sold in London. Nick began experimenting with jewellery. From a first mould he produced a handful of designs, which he showed to various shops and galleries in London. Before long, they began to receive orders from specialist design galleries. As demand increased, it became necessary to find a workshop. Through the local council they found some premises at £3 per week, on a short lease. Business expanded and they spent a few hundred pounds on improvements and materials for the workshop. The next big step forward was a magazine offer of a necklace and brooches which proved a real test of their organisation. 1,600 replies were received, and orders had to be dealt with and dispatched quickly. Their income from this venture went towards the lease for the present premises – a shop/gallery with a flat and workshop. Cicada designs have become something of a success, but the small, personal business atmosphere is something Pat and Nick wish to maintain. They have been offered orders for mass-produced items, but they are reluctant to be involved in a big business enterprise which would mean expansion, more staff and a possible remoteness from the production side.

Chapter 7

Other Careers Involving Art and Design

Arts Administration

Arts administrators are professionals involved in the publicity, promotion and organisation of artistic events of all kinds. Let us look at who the arts administrators are, where they are employed, and some examples of the kinds of work they are involved in.

Arts Administration and the Qualities Required

Some arts administrators are graduates from arts disciplines such as fine art or art history, but equally, graduates from any subject – engineering, science, social studies and humanities – have entered this area of work. Most graduates will have had experience while at college, or after graduation, of organising performing or artistic activities and events; for example voluntary work at a local arts centre, helping to set up an exhibition, helping to run a college arts festival, and organising drama productions.

Other arts administrators may have had training or work experience in other fields after leaving school, and have become involved in administration of the arts in their spare time, with amateur theatre groups, in festivals, etc.

So many different skills can be useful, even essential, in arts administration: accountancy, bookkeeping, publicity and public relations, journalism, typing, secretarial skills, catering management, and so on. A methodical and careful approach to organisational work is needed, a creative flair and enthusiasm. An exhibition officer in a college art gallery who once worked as a salesman for a textile company said: 'I hated the sales job, but please note, the training in basic admin was to stand me in good stead. Whatever you believe to the contrary, exhibitions need systems!'

Some, if not all, of the skills mentioned above may be required in any one job. In addition, interest in and knowledge of the art form with which you wish to work is expected. Some jobs may be specialist, ie information officer or publicity officer for an arts association or theatre, where experience of journalism and knowledge of publicity are an asset. An assistant in a small gallery, on the other hand, said of her job: 'There's just me and the gallery owner. I do everything from making tea to fending off the creditors. I'm responsible for all bookings, arranging transport for artworks, all the paperwork involved, sales, hanging works, invigilating in the gallery, doing the accounts, cleaning, visiting some of the artists on our books, and on occasion I have been known to do the gallery owner's shopping when he's busy. I would certainly not describe my job as routine or boring!'

One vital point: the arts administrator must have an understanding of the needs of creative artists, whether actors, dancers, visual artists or musicians. It is not a job for the frustrated artist or performer seeking to satisfy his or her own creative needs, though a creative approach is needed to help create the right atmosphere, initiate the right kind of events and satisfy the needs of the artist/performer and those who come to see performances and exhibitions.

Where Do Arts Administrators Work?

The Arts Council. Its chief role is to administer government aid to the arts, and there are relatively few jobs at their headquarters. The Officers in Literature, Music, Drama and Visual Arts have experience and qualifications in their own specialised fields. There are a few assistant administrative and secretarial positions for which competition is fierce.

The Crafts Council performs a similar function to the Arts Council, but this is directed to promoting and providing finance for the crafts, such as jewellery, ceramics, glass, weaving, and so on.

Regional Arts Boards perform a similar function to the Arts Council, but at a regional level (addresses p 121), administering funding for the arts and for the Crafts Council, organising publicity of the arts, liaising with local authorities, supporting and promoting artists, performers and craftspeople in the area. There are posts as drama officers, crafts officers, community arts officers. These involve committee work, receiving grant applications, liaising with local societies, art groups, and sometimes colleges. There may also be public relations and publicity posts, administrative assistant and secretarial jobs.

Arts centres, theatres, ballet, opera, concert halls. Where posts exist in stage management, front-of-house management, publicity, accounts, and so on. As well as managing and organising programmes of events, administrators meet the needs of resident and visiting companies, and there is often the general maintenance and care of the building to consider, bars, catering, general office work, and so on. Community theatre groups, touring companies and orchestras may also employ arts administrators.

Community arts is mentioned on p 81. There is a role for those with administrative skills to work in this field, on a permanent, part-time or voluntary basis.

Art and craft galleries and shops. Opportunities may exist in national and provincial galleries for exhibition organisers and publicity officers, and administrators in private galleries. Some galleries run by universities employ full-time or part-time exhibition staff.

Artists. A handful of artists employ personal assistants or general dogsbodies to do the accounts, answer the phone, arrange exhibitions, pack up artworks for travelling, and generally organise things in order to leave the artists free to pursue their work.

Arts festivals. Many cities and towns throughout the country have annual festivals of art events, performances and exhibitions. Some of the larger festivals employ full-time or part-time staff, and extra casual staff may be taken on when the time of the festival draws near. The Arts Council publishes a list of festivals and their dates each year which may be obtained from Dillons Arts Bookshop in Covent Garden, London.

Local authorities run museums and art galleries (see museums, p 89), leisure and amenity centres, conference centres, recreation and sports complexes where there may be careers in municipal entertainment, recreation and leisure management. In addition, some local authorities employ arts officers who liaise with Regional Arts Boards and arts societies in the locality.

Private Galleries. There are many privately owned and run galleries in most major cities, dealing with a portfolio of artists for whom they sell and organise exhibitions, publicity, etc. The famous area in London for private galleries is Cork Street, overspilling into New Bond Street and around Burlington Arcade, though numerous others exist. You may wish to target a gallery that handles a favourite artist's work, or school of work, of which you are knowledgeable or interested in.

Case Study

Peter is the Technical Manager of a London gallery

'In total I spent seven years at art college, the first year being a vigorous and varied Art and Design Foundation course at Derby. By the end of this, I'd decided on the direction of fine art.

'I took a break for a couple of years to work and gain commercial experience. I spent one year at a design company specialising in corporate identity and packaging and the second year doing voluntary work at two art galleries.

'I embarked next on a four-year Fine Art course at Newcastle which I found fairly ideal, being suited to the type of student who was very highly motivated.

'This was succeeded by two years on an MA Fine Arts course at Reading, which was good, being so opposite in approach to Newcastle – I felt as though I had the benefit of two very different philosophies.

'It was during these two years that I started working part-time at a commercial art gallery in London, as I was commuting from there to Reading at the time. I can definitely say that, in retrospect, the voluntary work first started four to five years before was invaluable in getting this work.

'I am working there full-time now as the technical manager, working on all transport and shipping administration, as well as sorting out the problems that occur on installing each new show.

'The job is constantly busy and often very stressful and demanding, requiring a careful balance between office and practical work. I enjoy the varied mix of tasks and the fact that new challenges arise constantly. One shouldn't enter this field with the expectation of great pay: the best rewards lie in working alongside the artists, promoting their work and understanding the structure behind a commercial fine art operation.'

Training

For those thinking of entering arts administration, the advice generally given is to get some experience first, and it may be important to gain some extra skills and put these into practice before looking for your first job. It is useful, anyhow, to test out your commitment to this type of work, so that you are better equipped and have more to offer when applying for your first job. Secretarial skills and training are very useful. Many arts administrators have begun their careers with a secretarial post in an arts organisation. Others may do box-office work, be assistant stage managers, administrative assistant, and so on. There are two full-time courses of professional training in arts administration, run in conjunction with the Arts Council, at the City University's Centre for Arts. Both are postgraduate or post-experience courses; therefore applicants have normally already had some related work experience. Some arts administrators may work for professional qualifications in the field of museums and art galleries, public relations, public administration, recreation management, management studies, accountancy, and so on.

Career Prospects

Vacancies in arts administration attract large numbers of applications. Salaries, especially at the beginning, are not high but the infinite variety, the scope for developing individual jobs and the special satisfactions achieved, make arts administration an exciting field in which to work.

Finding a Job

The Creative and Media Appointments pages of the *Guardian* and other periodicals and newspapers listed in Chapter 10 are the main sources for vacancies. Some entrants to arts administration may be offered a full-time job as a result of doing voluntary work in the same arts organisation. Speculative applications to arts organisations may well result in an interview.

Art Therapy

Art therapy is still a relatively new profession, and is allied to other remedial therapies, occupational, music and drama therapy. Art therapy has a role to play as a healing aid in improving the condition and often the quality of life for hospital patients or people with terminal or long-term illnesses, those in psychiatric care, the mentally and physically handicapped, and those receiving remedial tuition in schools.

Art therapy may be used as an interpretational aid. For example, psychiatric patients may find it easier to express feelings and emotions visually through painting or working with clay and wood, rather than verbally. Art therapists work alongside psychiatrists and psychotherapists and encourage patients to express themselves. As well as being good teachers and facilitators, art therapists must therefore have an understanding of psychopathology, which is studied as part of art therapy training. In addition to finding employment in hospitals, art therapists work in special schools for the mentally and physically subnormal as art teachers, using art in a number of ways – as a means of communication, in assessment, and as a way of encouraging creativity. They may also be employed as craft instructors in social services day centres for the mentally and physically handicapped.

Entry Qualifications and Training

Most entrants to art therapy are graduates, usually in art and design subjects, and occasionally in other subjects such as education, sociology or psychology where there is also evidence of artistic ability. In order to qualify as an art therapist there are courses of professional training which may be entered by graduates usually after some relevant experience (see Part 2).

There are a number of ways in which experience may be gained. Some people may do voluntary work in hospitals or day centres while still at college. One graduate gained some art therapy experience by writing to her local hospital enquiring about posts. She was offered a job as an art therapist which she did for one year. 'There is much job satisfaction – loads of responsibility to the patients, many tasks involved – creative activities, office work, liaising between school kids, social workers, psychotherapists, doctors and nurses. There's scope for ingenuity, but little of my own creativity at present.' She is now doing a one-year teacher-training course. Nursing experience is also a useful way of gaining insight into the work and working environment.

Another route to art therapy is after teacher training and a period of teaching experience in art subjects in ordinary schools, when the teacher's interests may incline towards more remedial and specialist work. This may then be followed by an art therapy course. It is also possible to combine a postgraduate teacher-training course with art therapy training. One or two such courses exist.

Here are some comments from a fine art graduate: 'I am doing a PGCE in Art Education and Art Therapy, which I entered in the September after leaving my first degree course in fine art. I will become a qualified graduate teacher and a registered art therapist. I do not wish to pursue teaching. On the course I have held placements in a children's hospital (as teacher), an inner city multi-racial comprehensive school, two adult psychiatric hospitals (as art therapist), and at an adolescent assessment centre (as art therapist and teacher). The course lectures include psychotherapy, psychiatry, psychology, sociology, eduction and philosophy. The course is geared towards group psychotherapy workshops – towards a fuller awareness and understanding of oneself. I find the work very satisfying and creative, and I like the variety. The psychiatric experience has been very useful, especially in psychiatric hospitals where I have worked as an art therapist. After the course finishes I have been accepted for a post as trainee social worker. In the future I hope to return to art therapy in psychiatric hospitals part-time.'

Obtaining a first job, particularly one which is well paid, can often prove difficult. A recently trained art therapist was offered a job as an occupational therapy aide but instead took a post as a teacher in a special school – where she was able to earn £2,500 pa more. Pay varies considerably throughout art therapy, mainly because of the variety of employers: the Health Service, education, social service departments, etc, though some attempts are being made by the profession to standardise salary scales.

However, the personal rewards and satisfactions in this field of work can be enormous, as they are with many of the therapeutic professions. If you would like to find out more about art therapy, try to arrange a visit to an art therapist at your local hospital or in a special school.

Community Arts

For years, many artists and performers have taken active roles in their own communities and encouraged other people to express themselves through artistic means – by teaching, community work, adult education classes, and so on. In recent years, some of these artists and performers have established a new identity, calling themselves community artists.

At the start, most community artists were unpaid. They worked with local community groups in a variety of ways: setting up a community newspaper; helping local residents create their own play or music; working on creative projects with playschemes. The artist or performer became a *facilitator*, an *organiser*, a *teacher of skills* to people who wished to express themselves and their ideas through participating in theatre, music, dance, the visual arts, video, film, radio, crafts, photography, puppetry.

The number of community arts projects in the UK has grown from around 100 to over 1,000, with groups or individuals operating on a regular basis. Many of these now receive regular support and some finance from Regional Arts Boards or direct from the Community Arts panel of the Arts Council of Great Britain, from local authorities or charities, though with present public expenditure cuts the future of many projects may be uncertain. Here are some examples of the ways in which community artists work and the projects they may set up or become involved with:

- a community arts centre with its own premises, often in inner cities, may have been set up by volunteers to provide premises for play activities for children, or a community centre for social activities. Once established, permanent and salaried posts may be created. Workers and volunteers may help run community festivals; arts/craft classes; theatre groups; dance; provide printing facilities for local clubs or pressure groups to print their own posters etc; your club activities, often with support of social services departments.
- summer playschemes; adventure playgrounds.
- some local authorities and new town development corporations employ community artists for community development work – helping bring residents together; running leisure activities; teaching arts and crafts skills.
- some town artists work with planners and architects in planning the living environments in new towns.
- Regional Arts Boards may employ community arts workers in conjunction with the local authority to initiate projects in a given area.

Career Structure and Pay

Community artists have some kind of creative skill to contribute and many are all-round performing artists who have had art college or drama school training. Little formal training exists, though there are some art and design and performance courses with a social/community element. There are no rigid career structures or entry requirements and financial reward and high salaries are not a regular feature. Few full-time salaried posts exist – those that do are with longer-established well-funded projects. On the whole, many community artists find it difficult to see their work as a long-term career. Hours are irregular; community artists are badly paid or work on a voluntary basis; and there is little job security.

Full-time work in community arts tends to attract young, single people without commitments who can afford the personal involvement the work demands. In reality, community artists may pay themselves very little above a subsistence wage, often preferring to direct funds into buying materials, renovating community premises, and so on. Trained teachers, art therapists, fine artists, actors, photographers, dancers, drama students, and so on in other employment regularly make a contribution to community arts activities in their spare time.

Entering Community Arts Work

Involvement in community arts while a student or after college can have many benefits for the student (and for the community) despite the lack of career structure and scarcity of full-time jobs in this field of work. Many students become involved in projects and summer playschemes on a voluntary basis while still at college. Community arts can be a way of testing out skills and development confidence in a wide range of roles and activities, before deciding on a career direction. In the past, those who have worked with community arts groups have moved into youth and community work, teaching, social work, arts administration, and some have become professional community artists. Your Regional Arts Board can put you in touch with community artists in your area.

Case Study

Helen is a fine art graduate working in community arts.

'I left college, knowing I wanted to work in a community arts centre in my home town. I had worked there in college holidays, and they needed helpers so I began work on a voluntary basis. After four months the centre received a grant from the Regional Arts Board and funding from the local authority for one year. Two full-time posts were advertised and I was lucky enough to get one of them, as I had (I hope) proved my worth during the time I had been there.

'There are four of us altogether, two of us working part-time on a voluntary basis. We are a musician/photographer, a drama specialist, a graphic designer, and my speciality is mural painting. I also do puppetry and mime. I must immodestly say that our talents do not stop there. We all have to muck in and do everything from building renovation to general organisation and admin. All our activities are decided jointly by the committee of the community centre, of which two of us are members.

'This year we have helped to run a fund-raising bonfire night festival; an old folks' entertainment evening (for which I helped local kids build a puppet theatre and run a show); regular classes in photography, drama/mime, silkscreen printing; mothers-and-toddlers meetings; painting a mural at a local school involving all the kids; summer playschemes; activity afternoons at the centre for handicapped kids. We don't set out to impose our ideas on people, but we can teach skills so that they can interpret things in their own way.

'I live two minutes away from the centre, so I always seem to be on call, which is OK, but I don't have time for a private life. The community centre is my life, I suppose, and I don't feel like moving because the work is so satisfying and varied, though the pay is not so good. My future plans are uncertain, though I am becoming increasingly interested in working with the handicapped.'

Related areas of work: theatre design, arts administration, art and design.

Conservation and Restoration

The preservation and repair of works of art and other objects of value are carried out chiefly in national and provincial museums and art galleries; by a small number of commercial restoration firms; in some craft workshops; and by conservators working with private collections or independent museums. Objects receiving the attention of conservators and restorers include: works of art – oil paintings, sculptures, prints, drawings, etc; natural history exhibits; and archaeological remains.

Conservation and restoration is a very specialised field,

employing a small number of highly skilled people who have normally undergone a lengthy training in order to meet the level of knowledge and standards of workmanship required.

The Crafts Council Conservation Unit maintains a register of conservators and restorers, provides information about training in conservation and carries out research into activities central to a well-founded national conservation service.

What Skills and Qualities are Required?

Those involved in conservation and restoration usually specialise in this area of work and may be concerned with the practical care, cleaning, preservation and repair of objects. A detailed understanding of the objects, the materials with which they are made and their history, is needed. In preserving objects it is important not to let the artistic skill of the restorer influence the appearance of the work in any way – respecting the original intentions of the creator. Conservators and restorers may also be involved in valuing and classifying pieces, working alongside art historians and archaeologists. Some restoration can take years of careful work.

Entry Qualifications

Those entering conservation and restoration do so from a variety of backgrounds:

- □ graduates and those with equivalent professional qualifications in the physical and natural sciences, art and design, art history, archaeology;
- □ trainee craftspeople in specialised fields, such as stone, plasterwork, gilding, furniture, etc can train to be restorers, and those with basic craft skills may be employed as technicians in museum conservation departments.

Increasingly, a scientific background is important – the Museums Association recommends a minimum of two A levels, of which one should be chemistry. A knowledge of chemistry or physics may be vital in understanding the composition of objects, in cleaning and in restoration. Conservators may also have to enlist the help of scientists with X-ray techniques and chemical analysis, in order to understand further the objects with which they are working. In conservation work you will find art and design graduates with an understanding of science, or at least a willingness to gain a working knowledge of this area while training, and equally, science graduates with practical and artistic skills. Some entrants to conservation work may have already completed voluntary work with a local conservation society or museum.

Training

In addition to the desired qualities and qualifications listed above, most people entering conservation work will undergo a period of training, normally in one of the following ways:

Courses

A selection of courses in conservation and restoration at colleges in the UK is given in Part 2. These can last from one to four years, and subjects and specialisms offered range from easel painting to clocks. The courses include practical work, historical studies, and in most cases science subjects as applied to conservation work. On completion of these courses, applicants may try for conservation officer posts in museums and art galleries, and with private concerns. Some of the courses have grants available in the form of bursaries or studentships, or students may rely on discretionary grants from their local authority. The course to which you apply will tell you where you should apply for financial support.

Trainee Positions

(a) ***Museums and art galleries.*** The national galleries and museums, such as the British Museum and the Victoria and Albert Museum and Area Museum Councils which govern museums and galleries in other parts of the UK, advertise trainee posts where those with the basic qualifications receive practical and academic training in conservation on the job. As with all vacancies in conservation work, only a few trainee posts appear each year. Trainees usually receive close supervision by experienced conservators and restorers in their practical work, and are encouraged to follow academic study, visit other conservation areas, and work towards the Museums Diploma of the Museum's Association or Diploma in Conservation, which can take several years. Applications to full conservation officer posts may be made after gaining experience and museum qualifications.

One example of a training scheme is that run by the Victoria and Albert Museum which lasts two or three years full time. Candidates require a relevant degree. It leads to the Diploma in Conservation of the Victoria and Albert Museum and of the Royal Academy of Art. Information is obtained from the Royal College of Art.

(b) *Other commercial firms* may give you practical experience, but there are no formal schemes to ensure that you will receive adequate training.

In addition to gaining practical experience, some short and part-time courses are available in colleges and may be run by organisations such as the Rural Development Commission.

Job Vacancies and Career Prospects

Few vacancies appear with the major employers in museums and art galleries, and opportunities with small conservation workshops and commercial restorers are limited. Training can take from two to five years on top of a degree or other relevant qualifications, and once trained, promotion from conservation officer posts to senior positions in museums can take some time as there is little movement from post to post in the profession, the work being so specialised. Salary scales can be supplied by the Museums Association and all posts are advertised in the *Museums Bulletin*. Other relevant journals and sources of vacancies are listed on p 128. As with many artistic and creative professions, personal rewards and satisfaction are considerable.

Case Study

Anna is a fine artist who obtained a post as assistant conservation officer (a training position) at a national museum. While at college and after graduation, she spent several periods doing voluntary work in museums, experiences on which she was able to draw when making applications for jobs later. In addition to her post, she has carried on with her own drawing and painting, has attended pottery evening classes, and is also a member of the City of London Archaeological Society which organises lectures and digs. She says:

> 'ACO is a training position, so the work involves about 70 per cent practical work with organic material cleaning, consolidating and repairing objects and textiles, at first under the supervision of a

senior, and now repeatedly making my own judgements about treatments etc. Thirty per cent of the time is taken up with lectures on chemistry and techniques. The work is satisfying and the results are usually very rewarding. The responsibility of deciding how to treat valuable objects can be nerve-racking, although advice is always available. The continual learning of techniques and culture is very stimulating. However, I should like more experience with metals or ceramics, or conservation on digs. Pay is adequate but not very good. Promotion is likely after four or five years. My future plans are to remain in this job and to take examinations for the Diploma in Conservation for the Museums Association.'

She adds that any kind of experience is very important when entering careers in museums.

Designers in Television and Film

There are numerous occupations in the film, television and photography industries, most requiring engineering, technical or scientific expertise and qualifications, and it is in these technical areas that most of the opportunities lie: opportunities in more creative areas are popular and extremely competitive.

The television companies, BBC and ITV, and the regional networks employ limited numbers of designers in several different fields. Vacancies rarely arise but speculative applications may be worthwhile. Work more frequently comes via individual programme-making companies, as more and more programmes are bought in. Film companies also employ designers, some of whom come from the theatre, television or from a relevant art and design course.

Set design. Designers for television and film are responsible for creating the right setting for production, in close consultation with the producer and director. This may involve creating scenery and selecting furnishings and props. In television, complex theatrical scenery may be required for a drama production, simple screens and studio furniture for current affairs programmes. Most designers and design assistants come from the theatre, or courses in theatre design, interior design, architecture, exhibition design, three-dimensional design and even landscape architecture. Creativity and an ability to represent proposed work in two-dimensional and architectural drawings are required. Special skills, such as model-making, are sometimes sought. Scenic artists work with designers in painting scenery and backcloths which require the ability to paint on a large scale, often working under pressure. Fine artists, painters and sculptors may find opportunities in this area.

Costume design. Includes the maintenance and cataloguing of costume, the occasional exhibition, designing and building costumes for historical drama, and so on. Fashion design or theatre design graduates may be employed, or those already with experience in the theatre. Much of the support work is carried out by machinists from the clothing industry.

Graphic design. See Chapter 5, p 50.

Film making and film animation. Graphic designers and illustrators may find work as designers and animation specialists with film companies. There are some companies and studios specialising in animation work. There are one or two art and design courses specialising in animation for film and TV and some are listed in Chapter 8.

Related Work

- ☐ Photography
- ☐ Film making
- ☐ Medical photography.

Museums and Art Galleries

There are many different posts in public museums and galleries, and for some, an art and design, or art history qualification is useful, if not essential. Vacancies do not appear frequently and when they do there is often fierce competition.

National museums are funded from central government and are mostly centred in London – for example, the Victoria and Albert Museum, the British Museum, and the National Gallery. Provincial museums and galleries are run and financed by local authorities. These vary in size from quite large metropolitan or county museum and gallery collections to small galleries and museums which may be attached to public libraries. In addition, many specialist collections exist, such as museums of industrial archaeology, rural life, costume, crafts. *Museums and Art Galleries in Great Britain*, a directory published by the Museums Association, gives a comprehensive guide to the collections and the museums and galleries in which they are housed. Private galleries and museums and commercial arts galleries also employ administrative and curatorial staff.

Entry Qualifications and Training

For most of the posts mentioned below, degrees or professional qualifications are normally required. Most museums will expect evidence of a commitment to museums work from applicants, many of whom will have had some experience through voluntary work while at college or after graduation. Many museums are willing to take voluntary workers for short periods. Voluntary experience in museums is also organised by the National Association of Decorative and Fine Arts Societies (NADFAS), and there are many amateur archaeological and conservation societies which may provide similar experience. Alternatively, depending on the type of post applied for, some experience in another field, such as arts administration or design experience, may be desirable.

Professional full-time postgraduate courses in museum and art gallery studies prepare graduates for entry to museum work. Once employed in a museum or art gallery, you are encouraged to work for the Museums Diploma of the Museums Association. Training for museum work is described in more detail in the publications listed on p 127.

Work in Museums and Art Galleries for Which an Art and Design, or Art History, Qualification is Useful or Essential

Careers in *conservation and restoration* are discussed separately (see p 84).

Assistant Keeper/Keepers and other curatorial staff are responsible for the acquisition, exhibition and explanation of collections. Where art, design or craft collections are concerned, keepers may have degrees in art history, or in art and design with a high academic content. These posts combine academic with administrative work, and applicants would need a special knowledge or at least interest in the collection with which they will be working.

Museum Assistant. This job may vary in content, from carrying out basic routine maintenance and classification work to responsibility for part of a collection, rather like the work of the keeper. It is a trainee position, while you work for the professional diploma of the Museums Association. Some museum assistants may have degrees or equivalent qualifications; others may be recruited with GCSEs and A levels. Art history and art and design qualifications are relevant for posts with collections in the arts, design and crafts areas.

Education Officers are concerned with education within and outside the museum, and in its relationship with schools and colleges and societies. This can include involvement with publications, organisation of holiday activities for children in connection with the museum, adult education, lectures, special touring exhibitions for schools and colleges, and so on. Most education staff have teaching qualifications and several years' teaching experience, together with a degree relevant to museum work, or at least a proven strong interest in the work of museums. Art and design graduates with teaching experience may move into this field of work.

Designers mostly work in larger museums which may have a design department, employing three-dimensional designers, model-makers, graphic designers and display staff. In small museums, one person may have to carry out all of these tasks – thus needing a wide range of skills. Art and design qualifications are necessary, and most applicants will have had previous design experience.

Exhibition Staff. Larger museums may employ specialists to organise and mount exhibitions. With an art gallery, this can involve all the administrative tasks to do with mounting an exhibition of an artist's work – for example, contacting owners of works, organising publicity, working with design staff in setting up the exhibition. Some exhibition staff may be involved in educational activities, such as organising lectures. Many staff in this area have art history, or art and design qualifications and proven experience in arts administration, while others may come from graphics, interior design or even architectural backgrounds.

Research Assistants may be employed by national museums to carry out specialist academic research in connection with a certain collection. This may involve some routine tasks, such as classification and cataloguing and literature search. With arts collections, art history degrees or art and design degrees with considerable academic content are normally required.

Technical Staff. Those with practical skills, such as carpentry or joinery, may be employed to support the work of museums staff. Only the larger museums may employ photographers whose work is mainly to do with recording specimens and scientific work. Photographers may be used on a freelance basis by other museums.

Other Types of Work. A very few museums and galleries employ specialists to carry out public relations or publicity work, for which experience in publicity or journalism may be useful. Sometimes administrative staff may be recruited to run museum shops, handling printing or materials, or sales work.

Related Employers. Charities, such as the National Trust, private collections and stately homes, may all employ staff for work similar to that carried out in museums, but job opportunities are normally very limited. Commercial art galleries employ staff for administrative, publicity and sales work, and their addresses may be found in the *Arts Review Yearbook and Directory*.

Job Vacancies and Career Prospects

Most of the kinds of post mentioned above are advertised in the *Museums Bulletin*, the monthly journal of the Museums Association, and in other publications (p 128). Local authorities are responsible for advertising posts in most provincial museums. It is important to note that the content of jobs with similar titles may vary from museum to museum and that the job advertisements and descriptions should be read carefully before applying. Public expenditure cuts have affected the number of posts in museums and galleries in the UK. Competition for posts is considerable, and promotion to senior positions may take up to five years or more.

Teaching

For many years, teaching seemed an obvious choice of career for the art school-leaver; it promised continued involvement with artwork; the necessary one-year training course was fairly accessible; and it was reasonably easy to find a teaching post. Now the situation has changed. In recent years there has been a dramatic decline in the number of teaching posts, owing to education expenditure cuts and the expected fall in rolls with the lower national birthrate, and it is no longer possible to be sure of a post after training.

Education cuts have also affected the number of posts in

higher education, particularly part-time posts in art schools, and art and design departments of colleges and universities. Practising artists, designers and artist-craftspeople have in the past relied on part-time teaching for a regular income and contact with colleges, but in schools particularly, those now entering teaching have to think more seriously about their commitment to the profession, knowing that there is no certainty of a job. Teaching has become an all-graduate profession. At whatever level you choose to teach, the possession of a degree is now a basic requirement, as is the possession of GCSE level English and mathematics – yes, for arts subjects too!

Some independent and state schools now offer residencies or part-time teaching appointments to aspiring artists/designers.

Secondary Schools and Further Education

What subjects are offered in art and design departments? Painting, sculpture, drawing, printmaking, graphics; increasingly – three-dimensional subjects: ceramics, wood, metal; textiles; and in some schools video and photography.

Craft, Design and Technology (CDT). The design and craft area is one of the teaching areas in which there are often unfilled posts. In recent years it has been generally recognised that a design sense, aesthetic appreciation, and the development of skills required in designing and making things, are as vital a part of education as the study of other academic and practical subjects. Many schools now have design departments which may combine what was technical studies and handicrafts, the emphasis being on learning through the use of materials. Design studies can include creative metalwork, ceramics, wood, plastics, furniture, textiles, technical drawing, and in some schools product design and engineering. The spectrum of qualifications held by teachers in this area ranges from qualified artists and designers to those with technical and engineering qualifications and experience. Students of three-dimensional and other design areas may find they have a contribution to make to CDT teaching.

Entry qualifications. Art and design teachers in secondary schools normally hold *either* (1) a degree in art and design, plus a one-year postgraduate art teacher qualification (ATC/ATD); or a postgraduate certificate of education (PGCE); *or* (2) a BEd or BEdHons degree with art and design as a major subject. Leavers from vocational art and design courses may have to complete a full BEd degree in order to enter the teaching profession. However, some ATC/ATD courses are prepared to consider applicants with art and qualifications other than degrees, and some applicants could also be eligible for shortened BEd courses.

Primary Schools

This area of teaching has suffered the worst cutbacks, and few posts are available. However, teachers in primary schools offer general subjects and have been specially trained for this age range.

Entry qualifications. Posts are held by BEds who have specialised in primary education, and graduates in art and design and in other subjects may enter primary teaching after a one-year postgraduate certificate in education (PGCE), having specialised in the primary age groups. The English and maths GCSE requirement mentioned above also applies to primary teaching.

Higher Education

Teachers and lecturers in art and design may be involved with Foundation, vocational or degree courses. New college-leavers are less likely to be considered for posts in higher education without postgraduate study or after some years' design experience, but it does happen. Artists and designers who have in some way made a mark for themselves through successes in their area, resulting in publicity, may find they are invited to colleges to offer fresh, young inspiration and input to a particular project or even to a course. Part-time teaching combines well with a freelance career, but as has already been pointed out, few posts of this kind are now available. A teaching qualification, however, is not essential and once some expertise is gained you can begin to circulate your CV to be put on record, should your particular specialisms and experience be required.

Adult Education

In compiling this book, information was received from several art college-leavers who had obtained part-time teaching in adult education. Some had completed one-year teacher-training courses after their degrees, and were unable to find full-time teaching posts in schools, or had chosen to teach adults. Others may be able to teach adult education classes without a teaching qualification. There are adult education centres in most towns and cities in the UK, and although adult education budgets have been subject to cuts, many classes exist in subjects ranging from woodcarving to trade union studies. Some classes may be self-financing, thus not having to rely on local education authority support.

How does one find employment in adult education? Sometimes a post may be advertised or it may simply be a question of contacting an adult education centre to see if they are short of tutors, giving some idea of what you can offer, or possibly designing a course which you are prepared to teach, and offer your services in this way. For example, a textile graduate, working as a freelance designer, offered a ten-unit course at her local adult education centre (one two-hour evening session per week) for which she was paid per session. The course was designing and making children's clothes. The centre was keen and had the facilities available, and the classes proved to be extremely popular.

The adult education centre may be able to help you cost out a course by furnishing you with average costs of courses, how much people are prepared to pay, what fees staff receive, abilities and levels of skill, etc. You could make an appointment to see the head or deputy to discuss preliminary ideas.

Adult education classes in further education establishments are very often run by existing full-time staff in the college itself, and there may be few opportunities for outsiders. The names and addresses of adult education centres to approach may be obtained from your local public library. In addition the WEA (Workers' Educational Association) adult education centres, community centres, community arts centres, youth clubs and so on may well be pleased to invite you to run classes on their premises maybe during the summer when premises and facilities would otherwise be unused.

Special Education

Teaching in schools for the physically and mentally handicapped normally requires a degree and teaching qualifications and several years' experience in teaching normal children. Art therapy training is also relevant (see Art Therapy p 79).

The general entry requirements for teacher-training courses, grants, and the methods of application are fully described in Chapter 4.

Some Questions You May Have About Training

What is a PGCE art and design? The postgraduate art teachers' certificate or diploma is a one-year course for art and design graduates intending to specialise in teaching art/design subjects chiefly in secondary schools. These courses combine study in education and teaching methods with periods of teaching practice in schools. In addition, some courses may offer special options in remedial teaching, further/adult education, art therapy and certain other special areas. Courses are offered at centres all over the UK and some are listed in Chapter 8. See also Chapter 4.

Art and design graduates opting to teach in primary schools or wishing to train for general subject teaching, possibly to middle school level, will find a PGCE (primary education) more suited to their needs than an art and design PGCE which is for specialist secondary school art teaching. In Craft, Design and Technology (CDT) teaching a PGCE is a relevant qualification, but some specialised PGCE courses exist in CDT teaching. It is important that you explore the differences between different PGCE courses for yourself so that you find the one most suited to your needs. Chapter 4 will tell you where to obtain details of PGCE courses (p 37).

What can you do to prepare yourself for a teaching career? It is considered to be an advantage to have other experience before entering teacher training, as mature entrants are often thought to have a greater commitment to the profession after other kinds of work. In order to test your motivation, involvement with young people – in community arts activities, summer playschemes, youth clubs, or adventure playgrounds – during or after college, is helpful, and good experience to have on your application form when later applying for jobs. Sometimes it is possible and even desirable to spend a short period observing or helping in a school. Contact your old school, or your local education authority, or the teacher training college to which you may eventually apply and they may be able to arrange for you to visit a school.

Career Prospects and Applying for Jobs

As has already been stated, teaching posts are in short supply, but if you are persistent, are prepared to be flexible geographically and in the range of subjects you can offer in art and design, you may well find a post. Additional skills such as photography, video, a willingness to help with games, clubs and societies, will certainly help your application. Promotion prospects have been affected by education cuts. However, if you are able to offer suitable skills in crafts, design and technology (CDT) this is a good area to consider.

The periodicals and journals in which teaching posts appear are listed on p 128. It is also possible to obtain vacancy lists from individual local education authorities, and sometimes speculative applications to colleges and adult education centres may be fruitful. For independent schools the Incorporated Association of Preparatory Schools, and the Independent Schools Information Service may be able to help with further information on how to obtain a post, though posts are advertised in the main teaching journals.

Case Study

Fine Artist: Sculpture and painting student, who completed an ATC and now teaches in a large comprehensive school.

> 'I teach in an art department of five. The other teachers do general art teaching and offer specialisms in sculpture, pottery and printmaking. I offer painting, sculpture, and also do some remedial work. I have my own tutor group in the lower part of the school; 11–12 year-olds. I teach the 11–14 age group mostly, but do some exam and sixth-form work with older children. I prefer teaching the lower age group – they seem to be so much more imaginative and free from inhibitions than the older children. I think exams can spoil enjoyment and curb creativity in art.
>
> 'A typical lesson might be on a theme. Last week with the third years, we talked about food and looked at lots of pictures to do with the way food is depicted. The contrast in the way food is shared out between starving and well-fed people in the world was brought out by the children. They started to paint and one group decided to work on a large collage, to be continued this week. Another lesson might be more technical – drawing the school buildings to look at the use of perspective. I try to run my lessons so that after I introduce a theme, the class generates the ideas and decides on the direction the lesson should take.
>
> 'I know some art teachers find teaching draining, and they stop doing their own work. It can be tiring. There are so many constraints in the way the school day is organised and in the materials we have available. I get a lot of stimulus from the kids though, and I am illustrating children's stories in my spare time, and working on my own sculpture in clay at home.'

Related Work

- □ Art therapy
- □ Community arts
- □ Education officer in museums
- □ Arts and craft instructors: some adult training centres for the mentally and physically handicapped may employ art and design graduates with, and sometimes without, teaching qualifications. Posts may be advertised in the educational press.
- □ Teaching overseas: unless you speak the language of the country in which you wish to teach, getting a post can be difficult.
- □ You could do a TEFL course (teaching English as a foreign language) and combine your art/creative teaching with teaching English. Contact the British Council, 10 Spring Gardens, London SW1A 2BN, for advice and information.

Part 2

Chapter 8

Full-Time Courses in Art and Design

This chapter lists the main awarding bodies, and offers a selection of the courses they offer in art and design. The full list is now so extensive that it has grown beyond the scope of this book. A list of directories and reference books is given on pp 126–129. Most are available in public libraries, or in school, college or careers libraries. Regional Advisory Councils for Further Education produce regional guides to courses in art and design. If you are making initial enquiries about first diplomas or Foundation courses ask at your school or local careers office.

Professional organisations supply lists of recommended courses, for example the Textiles Institute publishes a list of textile courses.

Information provided was correct at the time of writing, but do allow for change, and check that there have not been changes before taking action.

For *entry requirements* and notes on how and when to apply, please see Chapter 4. Entry qualifications, particularly for vocational courses, vary from college to college. These may be checked by obtaining individual prospectuses.

Key to abbreviations

A&D	Art and Design
C	College
CA	College of Art
CAD	College of Art and Design
CAT	College of Arts and Technology
CHE	College of Higher Education
CT	College of Technology
CTA	College of Technology and Arts
I	Institute
IAD	Institute of Art and Design
IHE	Institute of Higher Education
MC	Metropolitan College
SA	School of Art
SAD	School of Art and Design
TC	Technical College

BTEC and SCOTVEC

National Diplomas and Certificates

There are over 400 art and design courses at 135 colleges all over the UK, offering nationally recognised qualifications called BTEC National Diplomas and Certificates, and BTEC Higher National Diplomas and Certificates approved by the Design Board for the Business and Technology Education Council.

The aim of BTEC is to offer employment-related courses in art and design studies to complement the existing provision of degree courses. The standards are high and because employers have been involved in designing the content of the courses, there is often more practical experience, more day-to-day working in firms and on practical projects. Subjects include:

Art and Design
Visual Communication (including graphic design, illustration, technical illustration, typography, photography, audiovisual studies, advertising design, information design)
Fashion Textiles and Surface Patterns
Millinery
Footwear

Diplomas are more advanced than Certificates which offer part-time study for those already working in design posts. It is possible to progress from a Diploma to a Higher Diploma which offers an advanced, specialist training for a further two years.

Length of courses. Certificates: two years, part time; Diplomas: two years, full time, three years, part time or sandwich study.

In Scotland, the Scottish Vocational Education Council (SCOTVEC) offers two-year National and Higher National Diploma courses with equivalent entry requirements to BTEC courses.

BTEC National Diplomas in General Art and Design

Barnfield C, Luton
Basingstoke TC
Blackburn C
Cambridge Regional C
Cleveland CAD, Middlesbrough
Coventry TC
Croydon C

East Surrey C, Redhill
Eastbourne CAT
Falmouth CAD
Gwent Tertiary C, Usk
Henley C
Huddersfield TC
Isle C, Wisbech
Kensington and Chelsea C
Kent IAD, Maidstone
Loughborough CA
Newcastle under Lyme C
North East Worcestershire C, Bromsgrove
North Oxfordshire C, Banbury
North Warwickshire C, Nuneaton
Northampton C
Northbrook C, Worthing
Oldham C
Plymouth CAD
Portsmouth University
St Helens C
Salford CT
Somerset CAT, Taunton
South Devon C, Torquay
South East Essex C, Southend
Southport C
Southwark C, London SE1
Stamford C
Strode C, Street
Suffolk C, Ipswich
Surrey IAD, Epsom
Telford CAT
Thurrock C, Grays
Tower Hamlets C, London
West Cumbria C, Workington
West Thames C, Isleworth
Yale C, Wrexham

BTEC Higher National Diploma in Design

BTEC HND in Design. Most BTEC awards in Design have the title Design followed by the area of specialism, eg Design (Fashion). Courses are listed below under their area of specialism. The list shows a selection of the courses available. A full list of approved design courses can be obtained from: BTEC Information Services, Central House, Upper Woburn Place, London WC1H 0HH; 0171 413 8400.

Entry requirements: BTEC NC *or* ND in a related subject area, or its identifiable equivalent, *or* a BTEC ND or NC in General Art and Design *or* completion of a Foundation course in Art and Design *or* an A level pass with appropriate GCSEs.

Design (Advertising). BTEC HND: Doncaster Metropolitan IHE; Hounslow Borough C; Newcastle CAT
Design (Audio-Visual). BTEC HND: Northbrook C
Design (Ceramics). BTEC HND: Croydon C: Falmouth SAD; Harrow CHE; Staffordshire University; W Glamorgan IHE
Design (Communications). BTEC HND: Cleveland CAD; Dewsbury C; Gloucestershire CAT; North East Wales IHE; Northumberland CAT; Norton C, Sheffield; Suffolk C; Wolverhampton University
Design (Crafts). BTEC HND: University of Central England in Birmingham; Carmarthenshire CTA; Chelsea SA; Cumbria CAD; University of Derby; Kent IAD; NE Wales IHE
Design (Fashion/Surface Pattern). BTEC HND: Dewsbury C
Design (Fashion/Textiles). BTEC HND: Northbrook C
Design (Film and Television). BTEC HND: Bournemouth and Poole CAD; Gwent CHE
Design (Industrial Design). BTEC HND: Bournemouth and Poole CAD; Carmarthenshire CTA; Chelsea CAD; Colchester I, Southampton IHE
Design (Interior Design). BTEC HND: London Guildhall University
Design (Jewellery). BTEC HND: Epsom SAD
Design (Packaging). BTEC HND: Swindon C
Design (Retail and Exhibition Design). BTEC HND: London C of Printing & Distributive Trades; Salford CT
Design (Textiles). BTEC HND: Chelsea SA; Cleveland CAD; University of Derby; Huddersfield University; Somerset CAT
Design (Typography). BTEC HND: London C of Printing & Distributive Trades.

SCOTVEC (Scotland)
SCOTVEC HNC. Arts Administration; Arts Management; Art and Design; Fine Art; Graphic Design; Graphic Reproduction; Graphics and Illustration; Interior Design; Scientific and Technical Graphics; Public Art; Spatial Design; Spatial Design (Interior Design); Spatial Design (Retail Design); Technical Graphics
SCOTVEC HND. Arts Administration; Arts Management; Graphics Design; Graphics and Illustration; Interior Design; Spatial Design; Spatial Design (Interior Design); Spatial Design (Retail Design); Technical Graphics
A range of National Certificate Modules is available within this sector. National Certificate Modules are offered at a variety of centres.

Northern Ireland
Foundation Course in Art and Design: 1 yr FT at School of Foundation and Integrated Studies, Jordanstown
Ulster University Postgraduate: Advanced Diploma in Art and Design, 1 yr FT/2yrs PT.

National Council for Vocational Qualifications

NVQs offered in:
- **Level 2**: Exhibition Design; Fashion Design; Furniture Design; Graphic Design; Interior Design
- **Level 3**: Design
- **Level 4**: Design.

SVQs offered in:
- **Level 2**: Ceramics Design; Constructed Textile Design; Exhibition Design; Fashion Design; Furniture Design; Graphic Design; Interior Design; Product Design; Surface Pattern Textile Design
- **Level 3**: Design
- **Level 4**: Design.

City & Guilds

7900 Creative Studies: Preparing Working Designs, plus one of the following craft options: Soft Furnishing; Upholstery; Fashion; Embroidery; Sugarcraft; Flower Arranging; Machine Knitting; Hand Knitting; Interior Decorative Techniques; Ceramics;

Patchwork and Quilting; Lacemaking; Crochet; GNVQ in Art and Design.

RSA Examinations Board

Art and Design GNVQ (available at Foundation, Intermediate and Advanced levels).

Examinations Conducted by the Regional Examining Bodies

CENTRAL (North West Regional Association of Education Authorities)

Art and Design Foundation Course; Certificate in Art and Craft Studies; Design Skills (vocationally related); Graphic Technology

Yorkshire and Humberside Association for Further and Higher Education

Certificate in Foundation Studies in Art and Design

EMFEC (formerly East Midlands Further Education Council)

Design and Visual Studies; Computer Aided Art and Design; Foundation Studies in Art and Design; Graphic Design

NCFE

Introductory Desktop Publishing Skills Certificate; Advanced Desktop Publishing Skills Certificate; Basic Graphic Design Skills.

Other Awards

The Royal Academy Schools

Royal Academy of Arts, Burlington House, Piccadilly, London W1V 0DS; Tel 0171 439 7438

The RA Schools award the *Royal Academy Schools Postgraduate Diploma*. The course lasts for 3 years full time in Fine Art, Painting or Sculpture. Candidates for the postgraduate course must have a BA Hons degree or a university degree in Fine Art.

First Degrees in Art and Design

The following institutions (other than universities) provide courses leading to first degrees in art and design subjects. The names of the awarding body appears in parenthesis after the name of the institution.

Bath CHE (self-awarding for taught courses)
Bolton IHE (self-awarding for taught courses)
Bradford and Ilkley Community C (Bradford University)
Bretton Hall, Wakefield (University of Leeds)
Buckinghamshire C (Brunel University)
Cardiff IHE (University of Wales)
Cheltenham and Gloucester CHE (self-awarding for taught courses)
Crewe and Alsager CHE (Manchester Metropolitan University)
Cumbria CAD (University of Central Lancashire)
Dartington CA (University of Plymouth)
Edinburgh CA (University of Edinburgh)
Falmouth SAD (University of Plymouth)
Farnborough CT, Hampshire (University of Surrey)
Glasgow SA (Glasgow University)
Gwent CHE (University of Wales)
Hertfordshire CAD (University of Hertfordshire)
Kent IAD, Canterbury and Maidstone (University of Kent)
Kidderminster CFE (Wolverhampton University)
Liverpool IHE (Liverpool University)
London C of Fashion (Open University)
The London I – Camberwell School of Art and Crafts, Central St Martin's CA, Chelsea SAD, London C of Printing and Distributive Trades (The Open University)
Loughborough CAD (Nottingham Trent University)
Norfolk IAD (Anglia Polytechnic University)
Ravensbourne C of Design and Communication, Chislehurst (Royal CA)
Rose Bruford C, Sidcup (University of Kent)
Scottish C of Textiles (Heriot Watt University)
Southampton IHE (Nottingham Trent University)
C of St Mark and St John, Plymouth (University of Exeter)
Suffolk C (University of East Anglia)
Surrey IAD (self-awarding for taught courses)
Swansea IHE (University of the West of England)

University C of St Martin Lancaster (University of Lancaster)
West Herts C (University of Hertfordshire)
West Surrey CAD (self-awarding for taught courses)
Wimbledon SA (University of Surrey)
Winchester SA (University of Southampton)

University First Degrees

Aberdeen: MA Hons (Single, Joint, Combined or General) History of Art; History of Art–Philosophy or Religious Studies
Anglia: BA Hons Art History; Graphic Arts; Illustration; Study of Art; Studio Art and Art History; BA/BSc Hons Combined Art History; Graphic Art and Design; BEng Product Design
Anglia: *studied at Colchester I* BA Hons Design
Bath College: BA Hons Three-dimensional Design; Ceramics; Creative Arts; Fine Art; Graphic Design
Birmingham: BA Hons Combined Subjects History of Art
Birmingham: *studied at Newman C* BHum Hons Art and Design
Birmingham: *studied at Westhill C* BEd Hons Art and Design
Bournemouth: BA Hons Interior Design; Advertising Design; Computer Visualisation and Animation; Furniture Design; Product Design
Bradford: *studied at Bradford & Ilkley Community C* BA Hons Art and Design; Design Communications
Brighton: BA/BA Hons Three-dimensional Crafts; Three-dimensional Crafts for Production; Accountancy with Law; Critical Fine Art Practice; Fashion Design with Business Studies; Fashion Textiles Design with Business Studies; Fine Art (Painting, Print Making or Sculpture); Graphic Design; History of Decorative Arts and Crafts; History of Design; Visual Culture
Bristol: BA History of Art
Brunel: *studied at Brunel University C, Twickenham* BSc Art (minor only)
Brunel: *studied at Buckinghamshire C, High Wycombe* BA Three-dimensional Multi-disciplinary Design; Graphic Design and Advertising; Interior Design; Textile Design and Surface Decoration; Product Design
Cambridge: BA Hons History of Art
Central England in Birmingham: BA Hons Art and Design; BA/BA Hons Design, Media and Management; Fine Art;

Three-dimensional Design; Visual Communication; Fashion and Textile Design; BSc Engineering Product Design

Central Lancashire: BA (Hons) Design History; Fashion and Textile Design; Fashion Promotions; Fine Art; Graphic Design; Industrial Design; Product Design; Three-dimensional Design; Visual Studies; BA (Hons)/BSc (Hons) Combined Hons Design History; Design Studies; Art History; Art and Design; Jewellery and Silversmithing

Cheltenham & Gloucester CHE: BA Hons Fine Art; BA/BA Hons or BSc/BSc Hons Visual and Live Art; Fashion Design and Fashion Technology

City: *studied at Cordwainers C, London* BA Hons Design and Product Development (Footwear and Accessories)

Coventry: BA/BA Hons Art and Craft Studies; Arts Practice and Cultural Policy; Consumer Product Design; Fine Art; Graphic Design; BSc/BSc Hons Industrial Product Design; BEng Electronic Product Design

Coventry: *studied at Worcester CHE, Worcester* BA Hons/BSc Hons Art and Design

De Montfort: BA Hons Three-dimensional Design; Design Management; Graphic Design; Multi-media Design; BA/BA Hons Art Management; History of Art and Design; History of Art and Design in the Modern Period; Visual Arts; Fashion and Textile Design, BEng Electronic Design and Marketing

Derby: BA Hons Applied Arts; Fashion Studies; Fine Art; Graphic Design; Textile Design; Visual Arts; Visual Communication; BA Art Therapies; BEd Primary Education (Art and Design); BSc Product Design, Innovation and Marketing; Electronic Product Design and Marketing

Dundee: BA Hons Fine Art Drawing and Painting; Printmaking; Sculpting; Time-based Art; BDes Hons Design Ceramics; Graphic Design; Illustration and Printmaking; Interior and Environmental Design

Dundee: *studied at Duncan of Jordanstone CA, Dundee* BA Hons Drawing and Painting; Fine Art; Printmaking and Sculpture; BDes Hons Animation and Electronic Media; Ceramics; Constructed Textiles; Graphic Design; Illustration and Printmaking; Jewellery and Metalwork; Printed Textiles

East Anglia: BA Hons Art History; Art History and European Literature; History of Art and Architecture; History and History of Art

East Anglia: *studied at Suffolk C, Ipswich* BA Hons Art and Design; Design Studies; BA/BSc Hons Art and Design

East London: BA/BA Hons Art, Design and Film History; Design; Fashion Design, Fine Art; BEng/BEng Hons Integrated Electronic Design and Manufacture; BSc Product Design

Edinburgh: MA Hons Fine Art; History of Art; History of Art–Chinese Studies or English Literature; History–History of Art or Scottish Historical Studies

Essex: BA Hons Art History and Theory; History and Theory and Music; Philosophy–Art History or History; Sociology and Art History

Exeter: BA Combined Hons American and Commonwealth Arts–Italian; English–American and Commonwealth Arts; French–Fine Art or Greek and Roman Studies; Italian–Design; Italian–Fine Art; Music–American and Commonwealth Arts; BA Single Hons American and Commonwealth Arts; BEd/BSc(Ed) Hons Design and Technology

Glamorgan: BA Hons Creative Arts; BA/BSc Product Design

Glasgow Caledonian: BSc/BSc Hons Interior Design; Fashion with Business Administration

Glasgow: MA Ord/Hons and MA (Soc Sci) Ord/Hons Design; Fine Art; History of Art; BEng/MEng Design (Product Design Engineering)

Greenwich: BA/BA (Hons) Advertising Design; Fine Arts

Heriot-Watt: BA Hons/Ord Design; Painting; Sculpture; Tapestry

Heriot-Watt: *studied at Edinburgh CA* BA Hons Design and Applied Arts; Painting; Sculpture; Tapestry; Textile and Fashion Design Management; MA Hons Fine Art

Hertfordshire: BA/BA Hons Art and Design; Design Representation; Fine Art, Image Making and Design; Industrial Design; Two-dimensional Design; BEd Primary Education (Art)

Hertfordshire: *studied at West Herts C, Watford* BA/BA Hons Imagemaking and Design; BSc Hons Graphic Media Studies

Huddersfield: BA/BA Hons Interactive Media Design; Interior Design; Surface Pattern; Textile Design; BEd Craft Design and Technology; BSc Product Design

Humberside: BA Hons Fine Art; Graphic Design; Graphic Design and Media; Interior Design; Media and Graphic Design; Museum and Exhibition Design

Kent: BA,LLB Hons History and Law; History and Theory of Art

Kent: *studied at Kent IAD, Maidstone* BA Hons Three-dimensional Design; Fine Art; European Fashion

Kingston: BA/BA Hons Fine Art; Graphic Design; History of Art; Architecture and Design; Illustration, Interior Design; Fashion; Furniture and Product Design; Textiles

Lancaster: BA Hons Art History and Culture; Visual Arts

Lancaster: *studied at University C of St Martin* BA/BSc Hons Art and Design

Leeds: BA Hons Fine Art; History of Art; History of Art–History of Scientific Thought or Italian; History of Fine and Decorative Arts

Leeds: *studied at University C, Bretton Hall, Wakefield* BA Hons Art and Education (Art); Fine Art: Ceramics; Fine Art: Painting and Printmaking; Fine Art: Sculpture; Graphic Design; Performing Arts (Design and Technology); Fashion and Textile Design; Textile and Surface Pattern Design; Theatre Design and Technology

Leeds Metropolitan: BA Hons Three-dimensional Design; Fine Art; Graphic Art and Design; Product Design; BEd Design and Technology; Interior Design; History and Theory of Art and Design

Leicester: BA Combined Hons History of Art; BA Single and Joint Hons History of Art; BSc Combined Hons History of Art

Liverpool: *studied at Liverpool IHE* BDes Design

Liverpool John Moores: BA Fashion and Textiles; Fine Art; Graphic Design; Visual Studies

London: *Birkbeck C* BA Hons History of Art

London: *Courtauld I* BA Hons History of Art

London: *Goldsmiths C* BA Hons Design Studies; Fine Art (Studio Practice–Contemporary Critical Theory) extension degree; Fine Art (Studio–Practice–Contemporary Critical Theory); BA Joint Hons Art History–Fine Art; Art History–History; Textiles

London: *SOAS* BA Hons Art/Archaeology–Geography or History; History of Art (Asia, Africa, Europe); History of Art and Archaeology–Bengali or Geography

London: *University C* BA Hons History of Art; History of Art with Material Studies; History with History of Art; BA Hons Combined Studies Dutch–French or History of Art; English–German or History of Art; French–German or History; German–History of Art or Italian; Italian–Business Studies or History of Art; Spanish–History of Art; Fine Art; Italian and Design

London Guildhall: BA/BA Hons Design Studies; Fine Art; Joint Degree Subjects Design Studies; Fine Art; Minor Subjects Design Studies; Fine Art; Furniture and Interiors; Silversmithing, Jewellery and Allied Crafts; BSc Restoration and Conservation

London Institute: *studied at Camberwell CA* BA Hons Graphic Design; History of Art

London Institute: *studied at Central St Martins CAD* BA Hons Fine Art; Fine Arts; Graphic Design

London Institute: *studied at Chelsea CAD* BA Hons Design, Design (Interior Design or Public Art and Design or Textiles); Fine Art: Combined Media or Painting; Fine Art: Practice and Theory of Art

London Institute: *studied at London C of Printing and Distributive Trades* BA Hons Graphics and Media Design

Loughborough University of Technology: BA English and History of Art and Design

Luton: BA/BA Hons/BSc/BSc Hons Graphic Design; Industrial Design; Product Design and Manufacturing; Interior Design; Product Design; Visual Arts

Manchester: BA Hons History of Art; History of Art and Architecture; History of Art and French or German; History of Modern Art

Manchester Metropolitan: BA Hons Three-dimensional Design; Embroidery; Fashion Design with Technology; Fine Art; History of Art; History of Design; Illustration with Animation; Interactive Arts; Crafts; Education (Design and Technology)

Middlesex: BA Hons Design and Technology; Fashion; Fine Art; Furniture Design; Glass Design; History of Art, Design and Film; Interior Design; Metals Design; Printed Textiles and Decorations; Constructed Textiles; Fashion and Printed Textiles; Product Design; Three-dimensional Design; Visual Communication Design; BSc Hons Product Design

Napier: BA Interior Design; BA/BA Hons Interior Design; BA Graphic Communication

Nene: BA Hons Graphic Communications; Graphic Arts; Visual Arts; BSc Product Design

Newcastle upon Tyne: BA Combined Hons History of Art; BA Hons Fine Art

North London: BA Hons Interior Design; BA/BSc Arts Management

Northumbria at Newcastle: BA (Hons) Art History and Fine Art; Art History and Information Studies; Design and Design History; Design and Film; Fashion; Fashion Marketing; Fine Art; Fine Art and Photography; Graphic Design; Three-dimensional Design; Fashion and Printed Textiles

Nottingham: BA Hons Art History; Art History–English Studies or German; Furniture and Product Design

Nottingham Trent: BA/BA Hons Design Studies; Fashion Design; Fine Art; Graphic Design; Interior Design; Clothing Studies and Textiles; Textile Design; Decorative Arts; Theatre Design

Nottingham Trent: *studied at Southampton I* BA Hons Art and Design History; Design; Fine Art; Fine Art Valuation; Fine Arts Valuation; Graphic Design

Open University: *studied at Central S of Speech & Drama London* BA Hons Theatre Studies (Design)

Open University: *studied at NESCOT, Reigate, Surrey* BSc/BSc Hons Design Technology

Oxford Brookes: BA/BA Hons, BSc/BSc Hons, DipHE, Cert Fine Art; History of Art; BA/BA Hons, DipHE, Cert Fine Art

Plymouth: BA Hons Art History; Design; Fine Art; Language and Fine Art; Visual; BSc Hons Design Technology and Business; Three-dimensional Design; Medialab Arts; BEd Primary Education (Art and Design)

Plymouth: *studied at Dartington CA, Totnes* BA Hons Arts Management (minor only)

Plymouth: *studied at Falmouth CA* BA Hons Fine Art; Graphic Communication: Corporate Design; Illustration; Art History; Textile Design

Portsmouth: BA Hons Art, Design and Media

Reading: BA Combined Hons Art–History of Art or Psychology; Music–English Literature or History of Art; BA Hons Art; History of Art and Architecture; BA(Ed) Hons Art; Typography and Graphic Communication; Art and Design

Robert Gordon: BA Hons Design and Craft; Fine Art

Salford: BA Hons Design Studies; Fashion Design; Graphic Design; Spatial Design; Visual Arts and Culture; Design Practice; BSc Product Design and Development

Sheffield Hallam: BA Hons Fine Art (Combined and Media

Arts, Painting and Printmaking, Sculpture); Industrial Design (with Applied Technologies or Product Design); Metalwork and Jewellery Design; Three-dimensional Design

Southampton: *studied at King Alfred's C, Winchester* BA Hons Concurrent Design; BEd (QTS secondary) Design and Technology; Art History

Southampton: *studied at Winchester SA* BA Hons Art and Design through Drawing; Art and Design Through Drawing; Fine Art Printmaking or Sculpture; Fine Art: Painting, Printmaking or Sculpture; History of Art and Design; Textile Art; BSc Computer Science (Image and Multimedia)

South Bank: BA Computing and Product Design; BSc Engineering Product Design; BA/BA Hons Management and Product Design Studies

Staffordshire: BA Hons Design (Arts or Ceramics or Craft; Fine Art; History of Art and Design; BA Hons/BSc Hons/DipHE/ Cert HE Design Studies; Surface Pattern Design; Visual Arts; BEng/MEng Product Design

St Andrews: MA General or Hons Ancient History–Art History or Biblical Studies; Arabic–Art History or Economics; Art History; Art History–Classical Studies or English

Strathclyde: BEd (Hons) Design and Technology; MEng Product Design Engineering

Sunderland: BA Information Design; BA/BA Hons Three-dimensional Design (Glass, Architectural Glass); Arts and Design; Creative Arts; Fine Art; History of Art and Design; Information Design; BSc/BSc Hons Product Design Management

Surrey: *studied at Roehampton I, London* BA Hons Art in a Community Context; BA/BSc Hons Art in the Community Context

Surrey IAD: BA Hons Animation; Design History; Design Management; Fashion; Fashion Promotion and Illustration; Fine Art; Graphic Design; Graphic Design and Communication; Interior Design; Packaging Design; Three-dimensional Design; Printed Textiles

Sussex: BA Hons History of Art

Teesside: BA Hons Design Marketing; Fine Art; Graphic Design; History of Design and Architecture; Industrial Design; Interior Architecture and Design; Visualisation; BEng/MEng Design for Manufacture; Media Technology and Production; BSc Media Technology

Thames Valley: BA/BA Hons Design and Media Management; BSc/BSc Hons Computer–Aided Designs; Design Technology; Industrial Design; Packaging Design; Product Design

Ulster: BA Hons Design; Fine and Applied Arts; Visual Communication; BSc Hons Technology and Design; Technology and Design (inc DIS); Textiles and Fashion Design; Art and Design

Wales: *Aberystwyth* BA Hons Art; Art History with Art; Art with Art History; BA Joint Hons Art; Art History

Wales: *Swansea studied at Cardiff IHE* BA Hons Art and Aesthetics; Fine Art; History and Theory of Art and Design; Industrial Design; Interior Architecture

Wales: *Swansea studied at North East Wales I, Wrexham* BA Hons Design

Wales: *Swansea studied at Swansea IHE* BA Hons General Illustration; Graphic Design; Vocational Art and Design (Architectural Stained Glass) Textiles and Fibres; Visual Arts; BA Design (Three-dimensional Spatial Art and Design)

Warwick: BA Hons History of Art; BA Hons (with Qualified Teacher Status) Art and Design

West of England: BA/BA Hons Art and Social Context; Art and Visual Culture; Fashion and Textile Design; Fine Art; Graphic Design; Illustration; History of Art; Ceramics

Westminster: BA/BA Hons Design; Design and Media Arts; Fashion and Printed Textiles; Workshop Ceramics; Graphic and Information Design; Illustration; BSc/BSc Hons Design Futures

Wolverhampton: BA Hons Design for Communication; Design for Manufacture; Design for Floorcovering and Interior Textiles; BA Electronic Media; Fine Art; Three-dimensional Design; BA/BSc and BA/BSc Hons Art for Society; Computer Aided Design; Design Studies; Design and Technology; Floorcovering Design; Glass Design; Ceramics; Graphic Communication; History of Art and Design; Illustration; Painting; Printmaking; Sculpture; BSc/BSc Hons Computer Aided Product Design

York: BA Hons History of Art; History–History of Art or Philosophy

Higher Degrees Awarded by Universities

Anglia: *studied at Norwich SAD* MA Fine Art
Bath C: MA Visual Culture (Fine Art)
Birmingham: MPhil (Arts) History of Art
Bournemouth: MA Design Visualisation
Bradford: *studied at Bradford and Ilkley Community C* MA Drawing
Brighton: MA Fine Art Printmaking; Narrative Illustration and Editorial Design
Bristol: *studied at Cheltenham & Gloucester CHE* MPhil Art; Design; Fine Art; Philosophy of Art; Sculpture
Central England in Birmingham: MA Art Education; Fine Art; History of Art and Design; Industrial Design
Central Lancashire: MA Design; Fine Art
City University: MA Arts Management; Museums and Gallery Management
Coventry: MA/PgD Electronic Art/Electronic Graphics; Fine Art
De Montfort: MA/PGDip Design Management; Design and Manufacture
Derby: MA Applied Arts; Fine Arts; Graphic Design; Performance Sportswear Design; Textile Design
Dundee: *studied at Duncan of Jordanstone CA, Dundee* MDes Design; MFA Fine Art; Public Art
East Anglia: MA Art History
East London: MA Art in Architecture; Fine Art Studies; Studio Based Research; Visual Theories
Edinburgh: MSc History of Art
Essex: MA Art History and Theory
Exeter: BPhil Ed/MEd Creative Arts in Education; Visual Art and the Creative Arts in Education
Glasgow: MPhil Art History; Decorative Arts
Glasgow: *studied at Glasgow SA* MPhil Art and Design in Organisations Context; Design Theory
Heriot-Watt: *studied at Edinburgh CA* MFA Painting, Sculpture, Printmaking and Tapestry
Hertfordshire: MA Art Therapy
Humberside: MA Art and Design
Keele: MLitt Visual Arts in Contemporary Culture
Kent: MBS Cartoons and Caricature; MPhil Cartoons and Caricature

Kent: *studied at Kent IAD, Maidstone* MA Art and Architecture; Graphic Fine Arts; Illustration
Kingston: MA Art and Design
Lancaster: MPhil Visual Arts
Leeds: MA Sculpture Studies
Leeds: *studied at University C, Bretton Hall, Wakefield* MA Fine Art
Leeds Metropolitan: MA Art and Design
Liverpool: MA Contemporary Art
Liverpool: *studied at Liverpool IHE* MEd Art and Design Technology
Liverpool John Moores: MSc/Postgraduate Diploma Multimedia Design
London: *Birbeck C* MA History of Art
London: *Courtauld I* MA History of Art
London: *Goldsmith C* MA Fine Art; Fine Arts and Curatorship; History of Art; MPhil Art and Design; Design; Fine Art; History of Art
London: *Imperial C* MSc Industrial Design Engineering
London: *University C* MA Fine Art; History of Art
London Guildhall: MA Applied Art and Visual Culture; Computer Imaging and Animation; Design Research for Disability
London Institute: *studied at Camberwell CA* MA Printmaking
London Institute: *studied at Central St Martins CAD* MA Design Studies; Fine Art; Fine Arts
London Institute: *studied at Chelsea CAD* MA Fine Art: Combined Media or Painting; MPhil Fine Art
Loughborough University of Technology: MSc Design Studies
Manchester: MA History of Art; MPhil History of Art
Manchester Metropolitan: MA Art as Environment; Design by Making, Fine Art; History of Art and Design; Interior Design; PgC/PgD/MSc Design/Manufacture; Postgraduate Diploma/MA Art and Design Education; Communication Design
Middlesex: MA Art and Design; Design; Design Leadership
Newcastle upon Tyne: MFA (Master of Fine Art) Design; Painting; Sculpture
Northumbria at Newcastle: MA Design; Fine Art
Nottingham Trent: MA Design
Nottingham Trent: *studied at Southampton I* MA Design; Fine Arts Valuation

Portsmouth: MA Design; MSc/PgD Art, Design and Media
Reading: MA History of Drawing; MFA Fine Art
Royal College of Art: MA (RCA) Architecture and Interior Design; Computer Related Design; Fashion Knitwear; Fashion Menswear; Fashion Womenswear; Goldsmithing, Silversmithing, Metalwork and Jewellery; Graphic Design; History of Design; Illustration; Painting; Printmaking; Sculpture; Sculpture (Foundry Route); Tapestry
Sheffield Hallam: MA Art and Design; Design, New Technology and Project Management; Fine Art; Metalwork and Jewellery Design
Southampton: *studied at Winchester SA* MA Art and Ideology in Europe 1917–1968; Contemporary Art and Theory; Design History and Material Culture; European Fine Art (Barcelona/Winchester); Sculpture
Staffordshire: MA Fine Art; History of Art and Design
St Andrews: MLitt Art History; MPhil Art History; PhD, DLang Art History
Strathclyde: MSc Facilities Design and Planning
Sunderland: MA Art and Design in Context
Sussex: MA Tradition and Theory in the History of European Art; MPhil History of Art
Ulster: MA Applied Arts; Fine Art; MFA Fine Art
Wales: *Aberystwyth* MA Art; Art History; Studio Studies with Art History
Wales: *Swansea studied at Cardiff IHE* MA Art and Design Education; Design; History and Theory of Art and Design; MA/PGDip Ceramics; Fine Art
Warwick: MA History of Art: Venice and Europe
Westminster: MA Design and Media Arts; MBA Design Management
Wolverhampton: MA Art and Design
York: MA/MSc History of Art; MPhil History of Art

Diplomas Awarded by Universities

Anglia: *studied at Colchester I* HND Design
Bath College: PGDip Visual Culture; Visual Culture (Fine Art)
Bournemouth: Postgraduate Diploma Design Visualisation
Bradford: *studied at Bradford and Ilkley Community C* Diploma Art and Design; HND Design (Communications); Design (Photography)

Brighton: HND Design; PGCE Art and Design; Postgraduate Diplomas Fine Art Printmaking; Narrative Illustration and Editorial Design

Central England in Birmingham: DipHE Computer Aided Design and Manufacture; DipHE/CertHE Fine Art; History of Art and Design; Three-dimensional Design; Visual Communication; Diploma Foundation Studies in Art and Design; National Diploma Design (Fashion or Photography); Postgraduate Diploma History of Art and Design

City University: Diploma Arts Administration; Arts Management

Dundee: DipDesign Ceramics; Graphic Design; Illustration and Printmaking; Interior Design; DipFine Art Time Based Art

East Anglia: *studied at Suffolk C, Ipswich* HND Design Communications; Spatial Design

East London: Postgraduate Diploma Art in Architecture; Visual Theories

Heriot-Watt: Postgraduate Diploma Design; Painting; Sculpture

Kingston: HND Graphic Design; Postgraduate Diplomas Structural Design

Leeds: *studied at University C, Bretton Hall, Wakefield* PGDip Fine Art

Liverpool: *studied at Liverpool IHE* Advanced Diploma Art and Design Technology

Liverpool John Moores: Diploma Foundation Studies (Art and Design)

London: *Goldsmiths C* Diploma Art History; Fine Art

London: *University C* Diploma Fine Art

London Guildhall: University Diplomas and Certificates Art and Design Foundation Studies

Loughborough University of Technology: Diploma Design Studies: Digital Communication Systems

Nene: Diploma BTEC Foundation in Art and Design; HND Fashion; Graphic Design

Northumbria at Newcastle: Postgraduate Diploma Arts Management; Design

Nottingham Trent: Postgraduate Diploma Fashion and Textiles

Portsmouth: Postgraduate Diploma Design

Salford: Higher National Diploma Fashion Design; Graphic Design

St Andrews: Graduate Diploma Art History

Strathclyde: Postgraduate Diploma Facilities Design and Planning

Sunderland: Postgraduate Diploma Art and Design in Context

Surrey Institute of Art and Design: HND Jewellery Design; National Diploma Design; Fashion Design; Foundation Studies in Art and Design; General Art and Design; Graphic Design

Ulster: Advanced Diplomas (Postgraduate) History and Theory of Art and Design; Diploma of Higher Education Combined Studies in Art and Design; Design; Fine and Applied Arts; Postgraduate Diploma Applied Arts; Fine Arts

Wales: *Swansea studied at Cardiff IHE* HND Two-dimensional Design; ND Design and Print

Warwick: Postgraduate Diploma History of Art

Certificates Awarded by Universities

Bradford: *studied at Bradford and Ilkley Community C* HNC Design

Bristol: Arts History of Art

Cambridge: Postgraduate Study History of Art

Central England in Birmingham: Certificate Furniture Craft; Postgraduate Certificate Distributed Systems Design; Fashion, Textile and Surface Design

Durham: Certificate in Continuing Education Visual Arts; Certificate of Higher Education Visual Arts, Certificates Visual Arts

East London: Certificate Design Foundation Course

Exeter: Certificate History of Modern Art

Liverpool John Moores: Postgraduate Certificate in Education Art and Design; Design and Technology

Middlesex: Foundation Course Art and Design

Nene: HNC Graphic Design

Nottingham: Certificate Design and Craft

Oxford Brookes: Foundation Courses Art and Design

Salford: Foundation Course Art and Design

Sussex: Certificate Art History; Arts Management

Ulster: Certificate Foundation Studies in Art and Design; Postgraduate Certificate Applied Arts

Wales: *Swansea studied at Cardiff IHE* Foundation Course Art and Design; GNVQ (Advanced) General Art and Design.

Chapter 9

Addresses

General

Arts Council of Great Britain, 14 Great Peter Street, London SW1P 3NQ; 0171 333 0100

Arts Council of Northern Ireland, 181 Stranmillis Road, Belfast BT9 5DU; 01232 381 591

Arts Council of Wales, Holst House, Museum Place, Cardiff CF1 3NX; 01222 394 711

Chartered Society of Designers, 29 Bedford Square, London WC1B 3EG;

Crafts Council, 44a Pentonville Road, London N1 9HF; 0171 278 7700

Design Council, 28 Haymarket, London SW1Y 4SU; 0171 839 8388

Design Council Manchester, 24th Floor, Sunley Building, Piccadilly Plaza, Manchester M1 4BA

Design Council (Scotland), Ca d'Oro Building, 45 Gordon Street, Glasgow G1 3LZ;

Design Council (Wales), QED Centre, Main Avenue, Treforest Estate, Treforest, Pontypridd CF37 5TR;

Scottish Arts Council, 12 Manor Place, Edinburgh EH3 7DD; 0131 226 6051

Regional Arts Boards

Eastern Arts, Cherry Hinton Hall, Cherry Hinton Road, Cambridge CB1 4DW (Beds, Cambs, Essex, Herts, Lincs, Norfolk, Suffolk); 01223 215 355

East Midlands Arts, Mountfields House, Forest Road, Loughborough, Leics LE11 3HU (Northants, Derby, Leics, Notts); 01509 218 292

London Arts Board, Elme House, 133 Long Acre, London WC2E 9AF; 0171 240 1313

North West Art Board, 12 Harter Street, Manchester M16 6HY (Greater Manchester, Merseyside, Derbyshire (high peak), Lancashire, Cheshire); 0161 228 3062

Northern Arts, 10 Osborne Terrace, Newcastle upon Tyne NE2 1NZ (Tyne and Wear, Cleveland, Cumbria, Durham, Northumberland); 0191 281 6334

South East Arts Board, 10 Mount Ephraim, Tunbridge Wells, Kent TN4 8AS (Kent Surrey and Sussex); 01892 515 210

South West Arts, Bradninch Place, Gandy Street, Exeter, Devon EX4 2LS (Avon, Cornwall, Devon, Dorset except Bournemouth, Poole and Christchurch, Gloucestershire, Somerset); 01392 218 188

Southern Arts, 13 St Clement Street, Winchester SO23 9DQ (Berks, Bucks, Bournemouth, Poole and Christchurch, Isle of Wight, Hants, Oxon, W Sussex, Wilts); 01962 855 099

West Midlands Arts, 82 Granville Street, Birmingham B1 2LH (Herefordshire, Worcestershire, West Midlands, Shropshire, Staffs, Warwicks); 0121 631 3121

Yorkshire and Humberside Arts, 21 Bond Street, Dewsbury, West Yorks WF13 1AX (Yorkshire, Humberside); 01924 455 555

North Wales Arts, 10 Wellfield House, Bangor, Gwynedd LL57 1ER (Clwyd, Gwynedd, Montgomery district); 01248 353 248

South East Wales Arts Association, 9 Victoria Street, Cwmbran, Gwent NP4 3JP (Cardiff, Gwent, Mid-Glam, South Glam, Radnor and Brecknock districts); 01633 875 075

Professional Organisations, Private Colleges and Other Useful Addresses

Acme Artists Housing Association Ltd, 44 Copperfield Row, London E3 4RR; 0181 981 6821

Advertising Association, Abford House, 15 Wilton Road, London SW1V 1NJ; 0171 828 2771

Art Services Grants and Space, 6 & 8 Rosebery Avenue, London EC1R 4TD; 0171 278 5139

Art Workers Guild, 6 Queen Square, London WC1N 3AR; 0171 837 3474

Association of Artists and Designers in Wales, 54b Bute Street, Cardiff CF1 6AF; 01222 464 576

Association of British Picture Restorers, c/o Mrs Robinson, J H

Cooke & Sons Ltd, Station Avenue, Richmond on Thames, Surrey TW9 3QA; 0181 948 5644

Association of Exhibition Organisers, 26 Chapter Street, London SW1P 4ND; 0171 932 0252

Association of Illustrators, First Floor, 32–38 Saffron Hill, London EC1N 8FH; 0171 831 7377

BBC Corporate Recruitment Services, White City, Wood Lane, London W12 7TS; 0181 752 5252

British Antique Dealers Association, 20 Rutland Gate, London SW7 1BD; 0171 589 4128

British Association of Art Therapists, 11a Richmond Road, Brighton, East Sussex BN2 3RL (an information folder costs £5; send sae for list)

Bristol Old Vic Theatre School, 1–2 Downside Road, Bristol BS8 2XF

British Display Society, 70a Crayford High Street, Dartford, Kent DA1 4EF; 01322 550 544

BTEC (Business and Technology Education Council), Central House, Upper Woburn Place, London WC1H 0HH; 0171 413 8400

Byam Shaw School of Art, 2 Elthorne Road, London N19 4AG; 0181 281 4111

CAPITB Trust, 80 Richardshaw Lane, Pudsey, Leeds LS28 6BN; 0113 239 3355

Careers and Occupational Information Centre (COIC), Moorfoot, Sheffield S1 4PQ; 0114 259 4563

Careers Research and Advisory Centre (CRAC), Sheraton House, Castle Park, Cambridge CB3 0AX; 01223 460277

Central Services Unit for Careers and Appointments Services, Crawford House, Precinct Centre, Oxford Road, Manchester M13 9EP (for AGCAS careers literature and vacancy information for graduates); 0161 237 5409

Christie's, 63 Old Brompton Road, London SW7 3JS; 0171 581 3933

City and Guilds of London Institute, 1 Giltspur Street, London EC1A 9DD; 0171 294 2468

The Communication, Advertising and Marketing Education Foundation, Abford House, 15 Wilton Road, London SW1V 1NJ; 0171 828 7506

Computer Arts Society, PO Box 1454, Station Road, Swindon SN1 1TG; 01793 480269

Council for British Archaeology, Bowes Morrell House, 111 Walmgate, York YO1 2UA; 01904 671417

Designers and Art Directors Annual, 9 Graphite Square, Vauxhall Walk, London SE11 5EE; 0171 582 6487

Independent Television Commission (ITC), 33 Foley Street, London W1P 7LB; 0171 255 3000

Institute of Medical Illustrators, c/o Angus Robertson, Medical and Dental Illustration Unit, Leeds Dental Institute, Clarendon Way, Leeds LS2 9LU; 0113 233 6258

Institute of Packaging, Sysonby Lodge, Nottingham Road, Melton Mowbray, Leics LE13 0NU; 01664 500055

Institute of Practitioners in Advertising, 44 Belgrave Square, London SW1X 8QS; 0171 235 7020

Institute of Scientific and Technical Communicators, Kings Court, 2-16 Goodge Street, London W1P 1FF; 0171 436 4425

London Enterprise Agency, (Design Enterprise Programme), 4 Snow Hill, London EC1A 2BS; 0171 236 3000

Museums Association, 42 Clerkenwell Close, London EC1R 0PA; 0171 608 2933

National Artists' Association, Interchange Studios, Dalby Street, London NW5 3NQ

National Association of Decorative and Fine Arts Societies, 8A Lower Grosvenor Place, London SW1W 0EN; 0171 233 5433

National Council for Vocational Qualifications, 222 Euston Road, London NW1 2BZ; 0171 387 9898

National Society for Education in Art and Design, The Gatehouse, Corsham Court, Corsham SN13 0BZ; 01249 14825

Riverside Studios, Crisp Road, London W6 9RL; 0181 741 2251

Royal College of Art, Kensington Gore, London SW7 2EU; 0171 584 5020

Rural Development Commission, 141 Castle Street, Salisbury, Wiltshire SP1 3TP; 01722 336 255

SCOTVEC (Scottish Vocational Education Council), Hanover House, 24 Douglas Street, Glasgow G2 7NQ; 0141 248 7900

The Shelton Trust, (Community Arts), The Old Tin School, Collyhurst Road, Manchester M10 7RQ

Society of Designer Craftsmen, 24 Rivington Street, London EC2A 3DU; 0171 739 3663

Society of Graphic Fine Art, 9 Newburgh Street, London W1V 1LH

Society of Scottish Artists, 69 Promenade, Portobello, Edinburgh

EH15 2DX; 0131 669 0637

Society of Typographic Designers, 21–27 Seagrave Road, London SW6 1RP; 0171 381 4258

Sotherby's Works of Art Course, 30 Oxford Street, London W1R 1RE; 0171 323 5775

Textile Conservation Centre Ltd, Hampton Court Palace, East Molesey, Surrey KT8 9AU; 0181 977 4943

Textile Institute, 10 Blackfriars Street, Manchester M3 5DR; 0161 834 8457

United Kingdom Institute for the Conservation and Restoration of Historic and Artistic Works, 6 Whitehorse Mews, Westminster Bridge Road, London SE1 7QD; 0171 620 3771

Clearing Houses for Courses

Art and Design Admissions Registry (ADAR), Penn House, 9 Broad Street, Hereford HR4 9AP; 01432 266 653. Merging with UCAS in 1996.

Clearing House for Postgraduate Courses in Art and Design, Penn House, 9 Broad Street, Hereford HR4 9EP; 01432 266 653

Graduate Teacher Training Registry, Fulton House, Jessop Avenue, Cheltenham, Gloucestershire GL50 3SH; 01242 225 868

TEACH: Teacher Education Admissions Clearing House, PO Box 165, Holyrood Road, Edinburgh EH8 8AT; 0131 558 6170

UCAS Universities and Colleges Admissions Service, PO Box 28, Cheltenham, Gloucestershire GL50 3SA; 01242 222 444

Chapter 10

Further Reading

For addresses of organisations and publishers listed below see pp. 121–125.

Course Directories

Registration Scheme: Admissions to BA and BTEC Higher Diploma Courses in Art and Design. Registration Scheme, ADAR (Art and Design Admissions Registry). Lists the courses and describes application procedures up to 1996 admissions.

The Art and Design Directory, Mike Stallard, AVEC Designs. Gives details of first degree, HND and DipHE courses in art, design and communications. Updated annually.

The Degree Course Guide – Art and Design, Hobsons for CRAC. Lists courses in art and design and the history of craft and art. Updated annually.

Design Courses, Trotman. Starting point for those considering the study of a craft discipline. Describes courses from preparatory to postgraduate level, including teacher education. Updated annually.

Guide to Courses and Careers in Art, Craft and Design, ADAR.

Scottish Universities' Entrance Guide, Scottish Universities' Council on Entrance.

UCAS Handbook, UCAS.

Which Degree?, Newpoint Publishing Ltd.

Grants

Grant booklets are available from your local education authority and from the Department for Education and Employment, Honeypot Lane, Canons Park, Stanmore, Middlesex HA7 1AZ; Scottish Education Dept, Awards Branch, Gyleview House, 3

Redheughs Rigg, South Gyle, Edinburgh EH12 9HH; Department of Education for Northern Ireland, Rathgael House, Balloo Road, Bangor BT19 2PR, N Ireland.

Guide to Grants - Postgraduate Awards, Postgraduate Awards Division, HFE3, Honeypot Lane, Stanmore, Middx HA7 1AZ

Student Grants and Loans. Free booklet from Department for Education and Employment

Further Reading

AGCAS Careers Booklets. *Fine Art, Fashion and Textile Design, Two and Three Dimensional Design.*

Art, Design and Craft - A Manual for Business Success (1988) J Crowe and J Stokes, Hodder

Art World Directory, Arts Review - for gallery addresses

British Association of Art Therapists Ltd, leaflets on art therapy

Careers in Conservation and Restoration. United Kingdom Institute for the Conservation of Historic and Artistic Works

Careers in Fashion, Noel Chapman, Kogan Page

Careers In Museums, available on request from the Museums Association

Careers in Television and Radio, Michael Selby, Kogan Page

Careers in the Theatre, Jean Richardson, Kogan Page

The Creative Handbook, Reed Information Services - a directory of design consultancies, illustrators, advertising agencies, etc

Guide to Courses and Careers in Art, Craft and Design, Tony Charlton, National Society for Education in Art and Design

London Art and Artists Guide, galleries and sources of information

Making Ways - The Visual Artist's Guide to Surviving and Thriving, A Butler, (Ed), Artists Newsletter

Museums and Galleries in GB, Reed Information Services

The Professional Practice of Design (1983) D Goslett, Batsford

Running a Workshop, basic business for craftspeople, the Crafts Council

Survive, Association of Illustrators

The Textile Institute, various publications and course lists

Willings Press Guide, Reed Information Services, lists newspapers and periodicals

Working in Art and Design, (1993) COIC

Working for Yourself, Godfrey Golzen, Kogan Page

Writers' and Artists' Yearbook A & C Black, directory of newspapers, magazines, articles on finding an agency, copyright, self-marketing

Journals and Periodicals

Regular reading of the periodicals relevant to your interest is essential for keeping in touch with new developments, events, exhibitions, jobs and companies/consultancies/design groups you might want to work for.

The national press, such as *The Times*, the *Guardian* (creative and media appointments), *Daily Telegraph, Daily Mail,* the *Sunday Times, Observer, Sunday Telegraph,* the *Independent,* also advertise jobs in art and design, as do local newspapers from time to time. But you may find that some of the specialist journals are the best and sometimes only places in which to start your search for a job or to build your list of potential employers.

Key: W = weekly M = monthly Q = quarterly

A selection of those particularly useful to artists and designers is given below. See Chapter 9 for addresses. Items marked * are obtainable from newsagents.

Artist's Newsletter (M) (AN Publications PO Box 23, Sunderland SR1 1BR)	job ads, bursaries, competitions, grants, news, reviews: for visual artists
Association of Illustrators Newsletter (M) (to members of AOI)	
*Campaign** (W)	advertising, graphic design and other posts in design consultancies, publishing, arts, media, and marketing
City Limits (W)*	community arts, arts, mainly London
Crafts (Bi-M) (Crafts Council)	the magazine for the artist-craftsperson; some vacancies bursaries, workshop space

Current Vacancies (M) from univ careers services, or from Central Services Unit, Crawford House, Precinct Centre, Oxford Road, Manchester M13 9EP)	post generally open to graduates in all disciplines – some in the arts
D Magazine (3 times a year) (Gillard, Welch Ltd, Chester Court, High Street, Knowle, Solihull B99 0LL)	
Design Week (W) (St Giles House, 50 Poland Street, London W1V 4AX)	design appointments
Drapers Record 'DR' (W)*	fashion and textile design, manufacture, retail/wholesale trade
Fashion Weekly (W)*	fashion design and production posts
Illustrators (Q) (magazine of the Association of Illustrators)	illustrators
Knitting International (M)*	knitwear design – some appointments in design and production
Museum Bulletin (M) (journal of the Museums Association)	all posts in national and provincial museums and art galleries; includes keepers, designers, conservators
The Stage and Television Today (W)*	posts in theatre
Time Out (W)*	arts, community projects, media – mostly Greater London
The Times Educational Supplement (W)* and *The Times Higher Education Supplement* (W)*	teaching posts in schools, colleges, higher education, remedial and art therapy